The Complete VOCALIST

Mind, Body & Soul

Lee Risdale

authorHOUSE®

AuthorHouse™ UK
1663 Liberty Drive
Bloomington, IN 47403 USA
www.authorhouse.co.uk
Phone: 0800.197.4150

Published by AuthorHouse 05/17/2017

ISBN: 978-1-5246-6496-1 (sc)
ISBN: 978-1-5246-6495-4 (e)

Print information available on the last page.

Any people depicted in stock imagery provided by Thinkstock are models,
and such images are being used for illustrative purposes only.
Certain stock imagery © Thinkstock.

This book is printed on acid-free paper.

Preface

Welcome to this book. Whether you've found this book because you're a beginner or professional singer or simply because you feel you want to explore your desire to sing and develop your ability, this book is for you.

Some of the aspects and principles in this book may be familiar to you and others may be new. Some will even stretch the realms of your imagination past your comfort zone.

Our comfort zone is our own personal zone of acceptable confidence and understanding based on our current knowledge and personal experience. A paradigm is our belief system based on what we accept is possible. It's my intention that this book will help you change your current paradigm about what you feel is possible for you and expand your comfort zone greatly.

When I set out to write this book the majority of my understanding of the voice was based in science. Cause and effect. I found that if we use an exercise or technique and build it into our muscle memory, it will give an expected result. It's always been about proven results through practice and experience. My whole singing and teaching career to date has been based on this developing this experience. However, this book explores and expands the story further.

The purpose of this book is to shine light on an idea to combine the three aspects that I have found and observed produces great Singing. Mind, Body and Soul. For that reason I had to 'push the envelope,' go deeper into each area and combine them. I wanted to leave no stone unturned. I gathered case studies, gave interviews and became a journalist in pursuit of the truth.

I've involved people from many different parts of the world and from many backgrounds. Their contribution has enriched this book with perspective.

One thing I've learned through all this is that curiosity combined with an open, imaginative and objective mind can yield greater perspective and understanding. The fruits of this I gladly share with you here. Knowledge alone is not wisdom without conscious practice and experience. This book is based in both. Even the more taboo subject areas which have only more recently received more interest and acknowledgement through science. The world is changing as always and a broader mind is needed.

This book is also objective. What is the point of 'non-scientific' knowledge if we cannot make good use of it? Through experience we find that not everything has to be seen or published in science before we can make good use of it. Holistic natural medicine clearly demonstrates this. I submit that there are many things not currently accepted in science which are simply science that we don't yet fully understand.

In hindsight it will be always easier to see how I can develop and improve upon this book. I don't doubt that in hindsight I will encounter more ideas and feedback to develop this book and I welcome any such contribution to expand and enrich a second edition. This book will have it's own facebook page and forum so you can find further resources and share your progress in using the process and techniques shared here.

I've filled this book with my own sketches and anatomical illustrations to stimulate your senses and inspire you. I encourage you to keep an open mind and use your own practice and discernment to discover how you will make good use of this knowledge.

Enjoy this journey into your voice and have great adventures.

Acknowledgements

Written & Illustrated
by Lee Risdale.

Special thanks to Geno Washington, Emily Maguire,
Rosalind Morena-Parra, Kizzy Morrell, Laura Koniver, Teal Swan,
Marle Angelic Hernandez, Andrew Hambly-Smith, Clive Stocker,
Seth Riggs, Speech Level Singing International, Line Hilton,
Brett Manning, Stevie Van Lange, Max Weedon,
Matt Finch, Kim Lee & The Music Workshop, Georgina Hill-Brown,
Tim Goode and all staff and students at Bath College.

Thanks to musicians and bandmates Brett Lidbury, Ian Smith,
Terry Murray, Andy Urqhart, Terry Quinney, Sean McBride, Mark
Dixon, Andy Christie, Jason Newman, Rob Brian, Steve Sharp,
Malcolm Bressington and Stuart Nash,

Also thanks to Barry & Kay Risdale, Kellie Risdale,
Holly, Madison and Karen.

Reader, this book is dedicated to you...
I hope it will be a companion and inspire you on your travels.

Contents

Introduction

What you will find in this book.

This book is a practical manual for anyone who wishes to make the best of their voice and express themselves freely as a singer and performer. Within these pages you will discover a method and techniques to unlock your voice and with it develop your full potential.

I hope this book will be a companion you can refer to and keep you company throughout your singing adventures and for some, give you comfort and guidance throughout your singing career. This book is intended to assist your own transformation as a vocalist.

You and I will form a partnership right here between these covers and hold a light to greater understanding of your most valued instrument – your voice! An instrument of potentially great emotional and expressive power.

So... mind, body and soul. What's this all about really?

When I had the idea for this book I realised that I simply had to write it. It promised to be a journey of experience and discovery, struggles and successes, my own and those of my amazing students and contributors who each have their own unique voice and performance stories. Just as important as our successes are the struggles and the journey itself.

Why is it that we always celebrate success yet never celebrate the journey, the trials, hard work, pitfalls, disappointments and the will power it takes to succeed and overcome our difficulties?

I guess they're less attractive but they're vital in our learning and experience. I want to encourage you to celebrate all of these things as they're signs that you're moving forward and wisdom is given to you through every single learning opportunity and experience you take to develop yourself as a performer. During my own teaching, coaching and performing I soon began to realise that vocal performances need three key aspects, each of equal importance to develop a singer's full potential.

These are Mind, Body and Soul. Let's summarise these three aspects which are each of equal importance.

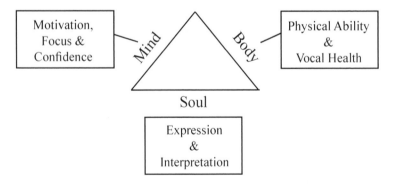

Mind *relates to*:
Motivation – The reason that fuels your desire to be a great singer and improve.
Focus – Is your ability to give your undivided attention, commitment and persistence.

Confidence - Realising and trusting your abilities as well as dealing with 'fear blocks.'

Body *relates to*:
Physical ability - Tone, vocal range, registration, pitching, articulation, technique.
Vocal health - Taking care of and preserving your voice with diet, exercise and avoiding 'voice-killers.'

Soul *relates to*:
Expression - How you truly communicate feelings in your performance.
Interpretation – How you communicate the intention of the author/writer/lyric.

So we can say that Mind, Body and Soul therefore translates to confidence, voice health and training, expression and interpretation. In this book I will illustrate how you can make good use of all three of these to reach your full potential.

I encourage you to watch and listen to your favourite singers and ask yourself if they possess all three. Let's call this 'the three point system.' When each of these is developed together and absorbed so that they become one complete package... your performance – You will possess the formula to become a great singer!

You might now begin to question which of these you possess more of - Mind, body or soul. One of them? Two? ...All three? Perhaps you recognise each of them but realise you need to develop them all and that's great. Let's clearly begin to grasp RIGHT NOW your initial motivation.

...To develop all three with a view to mastering them!

Part One

THE MIND

*"The mind of a singer – So are you ready
to look into the mind of a singer? This could be dangerous..."*

*"The most valuable asset to a Singer
is their intelligence and their intuition."
- Paul Rodgers (Rock vocalist)*

Chapter One

The great news is that scientists now agree that music lights up more of our brain than virtually any other activity. So it's sure to be good for your mind. Everything we do starts in the mind so let's set the stage and start as we mean to go on. You need to maintain a healthy mindset to be involved in music. A certain will power will keep you positive and strong to fullfill your goals. In this chapter you'll be concerned with developing a healthy mindset. Let's begin by establishing your motivation as a singer.

Motivation

Motivation is the meaning behind your actual desire to be a singer/ performer. It's about your love for music and being a part of it. At it's most intense this love becomes 'passion.'

When I started in music I had no great vocal skills to speak of. The same thing could be said for many Singers I've met and many of my voice students. What we did possess though, was a sincere love for music and that kind of love burning at it's brightest becomes passion. That's all you need to begin with. Everything else you can pick up as you go along.

Desire

Take a moment to ask yourself how much you love music and if you're prepared to make sacrifices to become a singer... perhaps even a great one! How much do you want to do it? How far would you like to take it? What would it take for you to achieve that?

A strong idea fuelled by desire and action will help propel you towards your destination and even bring that destination to you. So begin by stating your intention.

Let's establish your motivation RIGHT NOW... Pick up a pen and paper and answer these questions for yourself.

1. Why do you want to sing? How does it make you feel?

2. How hard are you willing to work at it?

3. Are you willing to commit and make sacrifices to do it?

Now take a moment to reflect on your answers.

If you want to be a singer purely for fame and fortune (even though it may appear as good motivation) consider how many singers actually achieve fame in the grand scheme of things.

Success is not necessarily just hitting 'the big time.' Success can be found at many levels and whether you are a busker having a great day or a Pub or Nightclub singer, a Cabaret or Wedding singer, even a local hero/heroine ... success and appreciation will still find you.

Are the doing it for the money/connection/appreciation or simply for the joy of it?

Maybe you are doing it to fulfill your desire to be creative and make music. To express yourself. Most importantly are you doing it for yourself and because you love it? ...This could be the best reason of all.

Goal setting

Having a clear goal is an excellent motivator. Let's use the desire and commitment you have established to make a clear goal for yourself as a singer. So ask yourself, what do you want to achieve? If the goal is a big goal or appears so at this time, that's ok. If it is, you can break that ultimate goal down into more manageable achievable goals that will feel more 'real' and attainable to you.

Strong evidence suggests that writing down your goals create a strong motivation and commitment to achieve them in your mind. Write down your goal RIGHT NOW. If your goal appears quite a large goal to you at this time, that's great. Aim high. Don't short change yourself. Next simply break this goal down into three achievable parts

My Ultimate Goal is _____

_____

I will achieve this by: (List 3 Steps)

1. _____

2. _____

3. _____

There are some people who feel they have problems achieving their goals. For some they struggle with following through to action them. Others try really hard and are persistent although for them it feels as though they somehow fall short.

If you were to fall short of your ultimate goal, please remember to take a look at what you HAVE achieved and keep moving forward. You can reassess your goal and change it. It may be that your ultimate goal does not necessarily suit you. So change it. In our culture there is a constant pressure through media to be famous or have substantial success in the Music Industry.

This may be what you desire. Or is it...? There are many levels of success and careers in the Music Industry so be flexible and don't let the media pressure you into some sugar coated goal which may not ultimately fullfill you. In saying that, if this is what you want ...then GO FOR IT! At any point you can re-assess and change your goal. If at any time you feel you've fallen short, look back at what you have achieved. Any form of achievement is success. Don't measure yourself against another's success. That only leads to suffering. Measure against your own development, step by step. Your own journey is all you need to be concerned with here.

Persistence

Persistence is your ability to keep working at your goals, no matter what obstacles, frustrations and disappointments may arise.

Persistence is as carbon to steel and that can hold everything together for you. Many singers who admittedly were not the greatest vocalists have succeeded in music through outright persistence in their music whilst singers who sought to perfect their art such as Sam Cooke, Michael Jackson, Beyonce and Freddie Mercury became world class vocalists.

Explorer Sir Edmund Hilary made his first attempt in 1951 to climb Mount Everest, the highest mountain on earth at a soaring height of 29,035 feet. That year he did not achieve his goal.

Climbing Mount Everest is extremely dangerous. Due to the high altitude he faced the prospect of lack of oxygen to the brain causing hypoxia, cloudiness of thought, headaches, sleeplessness, loss of appetite and fatigue. High falls and tight crevasses.

More acute signs of altitude sickness include dementia, poor co-ordination, delusions or even coma and the freezing temperatures mean a continual risk of frostbite. Many climbers have never returned from what was considered an unclimbable mountain. Despite this Hilary finally successfully climbed Mount Everest with his guide, Tensing Norgay in May 1953 after a seven week climb.

Compare the dangers Hilary faced to the dangers you face as a Singer. What is the worst that can happen to you in music? Yes, you can be rejected. You might receive feedback you don't like sometimes but these things aren't life-threatening. The Beatles, historically were rejected from every major UK record label before they met great success.

The trick is to view obstacles purely as learning opportunities in your development. If at any time a negative comes up, acknowledge it first, then view it as a pointer to something you can improve or develop that will enrich you as a Singer. The best thing to do is learn from it, make adjustments and move forwards.

Each time you react this way you're using these learning opportunities to guide you closer to your goal. In the same way as life itself is full of learning opportunities and you can either hide from them or face them head-on. They will strengthen you on your journey.

Persistence for a Singer is as carbon to steel. If you have the nerve to keep working at it you WILL be rewarded. So aim to develop resilience to any knock-backs or what you may feel as any set-back in your vocal development.

Keep your mind on what you want and don't let go of it. If it doesn't work one particular way, then try another. The results might be suggesting that a different tact is needed for you to succeed so pay attention to the signs and simply make adjustments in response to the feedback you're getting.

Persistence is an attitude. A commitment to never giving up. A muscle of your mind that you need to exercise regularly. So make it your habit to be persistent and you surely will succeed.

Persistence, persistence, persistence.

The Power of Receiving

Many people also hold themselves back unconsciously from what they want. I know... This sounds insane, right? But many people unconsciously sabotage themselves.

If this is you, you might need to learn how to be a good receiver.

This means that you have to be courageous enough to state what you want and act in such a way that you're open to receive it.

"A lot of people are afraid to say what they want. That's why they don't get what they want." - Madonna.

In her book 'The power of receiving,' Amanda Owen defines three steps to becoming a skilled receiver.

1. Accept all compliments – How many times have you rejected a compliment with some uncomfortable off-hand remark intended to display modesty or through distrust?

Instead we can just simply say 'thank you' and accept it as a truth.

2. Be grateful – Show gratitude for all you have and you are offered. Show appreciation for everything. According to universal laws it is said that when you make a regular practice of feeling gratitude, abundance will come to you. On my travels it's often said amongst musicians that you should be grateful and appreciative on your way up so that you don't get kicked on the way back down.

This is also a scientific principle supported by Quantum Physics which observes how energy behaves. You are energy and gratitude is a receptive state. Make a list of everything, anything no matter how small you're grateful for. If you make a practice of doing this by habit, it gets you into the receptive state which attracts more opportunity.

3. Be self-revealing – Don't be afraid to show people the authentic you. This is by default more attractive to others as builds trust that you are after all, human. Someone to relate to. This may seem a simple principle yet so many singers and performers hide their true self. They hide their light under a bushel. Some seek to present a very false un-natural self or an image which never serves them well long term and repels people and opportunities away from them. It may take more courage but being authentic will be rewarding in the long term both creatively and artistically too. However, don't let that deter you from 'acting' or putting on a show as a performer which we'll talk about later in this book. Vocal performances often have great elements of acting that are effective and entertaining. But offstage, be yourself.

Coaching

The benefits of coaching or receiving coaching for your singing can be huge. A tutor or coach will give you the advantage of their unique and experienced perspective. The mere presence of another conscious observer who is dedicated to helping you develop your ability is exhilarating to your progress. A good coach will enable you to fine-tune your vocal ability with the benefit of specific vocal exercises designed to build strength and flexibility.

It's also very important to find the right teacher or coach for you. A good coach should be working alongside you and you should share an understanding. Good communication with your vocal coach will ensure you get exactly what you need to progress.

The simple truth is that a good coach will give you honest feedback, solutions and encouragement that will motivate you and speed your progress in your singing. Their knowledge of techniques and good practice can be invaluable.

There are some things that all singers can do themselves to develop and there are some things that truly require the observation and objective listening of a qualified professional.

The important thing for you to do if you are getting coaching is to establish a rapport with your coach and let them know what you are seeking to achieve. This is your marker that will gain understanding and trust in where you're going and what your expectations are. If you don't feel a good rapport with your vocal coach then seek another one. You need to be comfortable and it's a partnership after all.

At the same time be mindful of not expecting too much too quickly and that coaching and training your voice is a process that involves some patience and commitment on your part.

A good vocal coach that you can trust is worth their weight in gold and a worthy investment of your time and money. The results of this commitment will be clear in your performance. You can make far greater progress, can sky rocket your confidence and will greatly reward you in the long term.

Chapter Two

Focus

'Focus' refers to your ability to give something your undivided attention. This means you will give singing your time and commitment. It also means when you're performing, your performance is your 100% present commitment and you reject any other distractions.

Focus also requires you to be persistent. It refers to you developing your ability to keep coming back to it and never give up on it despite any obstacles which arise. You will develop a resilience which enables you to bounce back from any problems you face and overcome them. So... ask yourself this question. How much do I want this..? If you're passionate about music, your answer will help give you more focus.

If you have problems with focus, let's consider all of the lovely distractions that modern society has to offer.

The Internet – *Switch it off*
Television – *Switch it off*
Mobile phone – *Switch it off*
Chatterbox friends – *Give them the day off*

Now you're ready to focus. :)

Overcoming distractions

The biggest challenge we face in this digital age of distractions is developing our ability to focus on what is most important to us and so you need to give your intention only to that which you REALLY want.

The most important way you can focus yourself is to remove yourself from any thinking about the past or the future. Be in the PRESENT moment. Quiet your mind and concentrate only on what you want to do RIGHT NOW. Focus on what you want to achieve and set about doing it ... Be persistent.

Will power

Having a clear, determined goal will help your focus and add fuel to your performance. For example: A clear determined goal of wanting to impress an audience and give them a great show can overcome any nervous feelings or anxiety.

Simply shift any anxiety feelings or worry into the focused power that accompanies your determination to succeed. In the same way as an athlete trains their mind to run a fast race, you can use the same technique to prepare yourself mentally in a positive state.

Scientists prepared a group of athletes for a race by asking them to run the race over and over in their minds and visualise a fast and favourable result. They then had them race another group of athletes who were not mentally prepared but just as physically fit. The results were astonishing as the whole of the group that had been prepared mentally were faster. They called this 'psycho-motor rehearsal.'

An Australian psychologist, Allen Richardson conducted an experiment on Basketball players making hoop shots.

Group A - Was asked to practice their shots on a basketball court for 20 days

Group B - Was asked not to practice at all

Group C - Was asked to mentally rehearse shooting through a hoop for 20 minutes each day

At the end of the study he found that Group A improved their hoop shot ability by 25%. Group B as expected showed no improvement. What was surprising was that Group C improved by 24% even though they had not physically set foot in a basketball court.

Therefore we can conclude that the power of the mind to visualise makes a significant effect on physical actions. Visualising your successful performance doesn't seem so foolish now does it?

Creative Visualisation

In Creative Visualisation we use the power of imagination to create a mental image of what we want to accomplish or obtain.

Some of the greatest thinkers in the world - Einstein, Edison, Jung, Carnegie and Goethe (the man with the highest recorded I.Q of 210) all believed in the power of the mind to create coincidences.

"Imagination is the beginning of creation. You WILL what you imagine and at last you CREATE what you WILL." - George Bernard Shaw (1856-1950)

Here I'm going to present how you can use Creative Visualisation to positively improve your confidence and your performance. Before I disclose the technique I'm going to tell you a little story of how I tested this.

The day before a music performance, where many of my students were performing I decided to conduct an experiment. I let my students know that I was going to try an experiment of the mind and needed three volunteers.

The three volunteer singers were each given clear instruction to follow to prepare on the evening before the performance. All of the other performers were not given these instructions.

On the day of the performance twenty singers performed in their bands all of varying ability and standards but all did quite well. However, among these singers there were three that really stood out both in the quality of their performance and the reaction they received from the audience. Can you guess which three these were...?

The next day all of my students were buzzing about the experiment and of course I then proceeded to teach the technique to all of them.

The following technique can be very powerful although it will work better for you if you get yourself into a relaxed or meditative state first (see meditation next). It's a state akin to day-dreaming, so you need to de-focus your vision or close your eyes.

Creative Visualisation Technique 1:

1) Close your eyes or de-focus your vision.

2) Take three slow, long deep breaths and continue breathing rhythmically.

3) Direct your eyes (whether closed or de-focused) slightly upwards, just above eyelevel.

4) Project an image of a movie screen in your mind. Upon the screen I want you to project the image of the view from your stage at a performance. It's your view from the stage as the performer.

5) Next, I want you to visualise the performance in action, the other musicians and the audience as you can imagine it.

6) Now move the movie screen slightly to the left. Now, see the musicians in action and the audience responding to your music in any way you would like them to. They might be clapping, smiling, singing along. Be aware of how this makes you feel.

7) Move the movie screen to the left for the final scene. Imagine and visualise the audience reacting with enthusiastic applause when the song has finished. This is a congratulatory scene of appreciation of your performance. Again, notice how this makes you feel.

8) When you're ready, count yourself out of the visualisation. Five, four, three, two, one. Now open your eyes.

There is something amazing about your mind's ability to set up scenarios in such a way that focus your performance with commitment and confidence that can really power your performance and influence the audience in turn.

It doesn't matter whether you understand how it works...or not. If you know what you want and you project that intention... it works... every time. Another useful tool here is in the use of Affirmations.

Affirmations are positive statements which have been proven to have a strong affect on the subconscious mind through constant spaced repetition and using this along with your imagination makes for a powerful mindset.

Creative Visualisation Technique 2:

Here is a another simple Creative Visualisation technique to try with your Goals or before you perform:

It's a simple three-step process.

1. Imagine your desired outcome. How does it look, sound, smell, feel?

2. Repeat a positive affirmation about your goal. Say it in the present tense. For example: "I AM performing at my very best ability."

3. Finally, imagine a congratulatory scene or a great audience reaction.

The emphasis in creative visualisation is on positive outcomes and this is the creative juice of realising an actual positive outcome and the polar opposite of worrying and expecting the worst which often invites your worst case scenario over for tea and biscuits or even a pint of brown ale before it kicks you in the behind.

You see, you become the thoughts you think in your actions and to others and these thoughts become your expectation and attract scenarios that reflect your positive state of mind. There are too many examples of this in action to list in this book. But for the moment, just take my advice and focus on what you want using creative visualisation. At the very least you'll remain positive which in itself can work wonders for a singer. But you may also be surprised how this positively affects what manifests into your experience. It's a universal law which when practiced regularly can bring amazing results. Why rely on luck when you can create your own?

The Benefits of Meditation

Meditation is also a practice which exercises focus perfectly. Surprisingly for some, it actually requires more effort to clear your mind of distraction and damaging self-talk than it does to simply allow it to cloud your performance.

If you would like to try meditation there are many free guided meditations available via the internet and especially created music to help you to develop a laser-like focus. It might surprise you to know that many of the world's finest singers and performers take advantage of meditation and besides it's relaxation and developing of focus it has been proven to have excellent health benefits.

***"An ancient cure may be the solution to a modern problem."* - Paul McCartney on meditation.**

The Silva Method is an excellent example of understanding how through science powerful meditation techniques have been proven to enhance mind and body.

In 1996, Texan radio repairman Jose Silva stumbled upon one of the greatest discoveries of the century. Silva already knew that reducing the resistance in an electrical wire allowed more electricity to flow through it (Ohm's law). In using this technology as a basis he wondered what would happen if you could reduce the resistance in the human brain. Research and experimentation that followed showed that in training people to function at brain frequency levels known as Alpha and Theta, levels of deep relaxation they showed surprising mental and physical benefits. From stress relief to enhanced creativity and intuition, accelerated physical and emotional healing.

***"Meditation is training and understanding the mind."* - Teal Swan**

Here is a Meditation centering exercise developed by the Silva method which you can use to relax as well as to clear and focus your mind.

You can practice this to relaxing music or you may be able to access the Silva Centering exercise on youtube or other social media as a guided meditation.

1) Sit comfortably and close your eyes. Take a deep breath and as you exhale mentally repeat the number '3' three times in your mind. Level '3' represents physical relaxation.

2) Bring your attention to areas of your body, starting with your head and gradually working down your body to your toes. As you concentrate your sense of awareness on each part of your body you will detect a fine vibration and a feeling of warmth caused by circulation. Release and completely relax all tensions and ligament pressures and place each part of your body in a deep state of relaxation until you are at a deeper level of physical relaxation.

Lee Risdale

3) Take a deep breath and as you exhale, mentally repeat the number '2' three times. At this level you will visualise a tranquil and passive scene. For example, a day out on the beach may be a tranquil and passive scene for you or perhaps a woodland scene. Take as long as you feel like to enable you to feel more mentally relaxed.

4) Next take a deep breath and as you exhale, mentally repeat the number '1' three times. Now count down from 10 to 1 and with each number allow yourself to fall deeper and deeper into relaxation. To enable you to reach a deeper, healthier level of mind, count from 1 to 3 and project yourself mentally into your ideal place of relaxation.

5) When you feel that you have spent enough time at your mental place of relaxation (without falling asleep) mentally count yourself slowly from out of the meditation 1 to 5. At 5 you will be full awake, feeling better than before and your mind much clearer... Centred.

The Silva Method offers excellent techniques to enable you to develop your ability to meditate well and many find this an excellent way to clear and focus their mind and much more besides. If you want to explore meditation further there are many specialist books and the internet has many free guided meditations and music to help you practice getting into this state or search for https://www.silvamethod.com.

This state or 'frequency of mind' we're talking about here has been described as Alpha level. A feeling in between awakeness and sleep. It feels a bit like when you're just waking up in the morning or day-dreaming. At this level of mind you're also able to influence your subconscious mind which runs 90% of the show and therefore get yourself into a focused state for your vocal performance. So when you're in this state you can use affirmations that will elevate your focus and confidence.

Interview with

Singer/Songwriter

Emily Maguire

How do you get 'in the zone' when you perform? Is it all about the songs?

"My songwriting comes from my heart so once I'm on stage I get lost in the songs and the message I'm trying to convey. But I have to really psych myself up to perform so I have a strict routine in getting prepared. Before I go on, I get very clear in my mind about my intention - my reasons for doing it, which are to uplift, comfort and inspire people with my music. This helps calm my nerves by making me think about what I want to give to others with my performance rather than getting neurotic about singing in front of a lot of people."

Do you warm up your voice before you sing?

"I use techniques such as sirening the word 'ing' very quietly to warm up my vocal cords and then doing scales using the word 'naw'. I drink room temperature water and a glass of red wine but I stop drinking anything 15 minutes before a performance. I usually have a bit of brandy just before I go on for a bit of last-minute extra courage. I try not to talk too much or overuse my voice to save it for the performance."

Do you have any good remedies for a sore throat?

"A honey, lemon and ginger hot drink is great but it's also really important to know when to cancel a gig if your voice isn't up to it."

How do you stay physically fit to sing? Do you find rehearsing & gigging is enough to keep your voice in shape?

"When I'm touring I do my vocal exercises every day and that enables me to perform night after night without losing my voice. I take Echinacea and Citricidal (grapefruit seed extract) to boost my immune system so I don't catch coughs and colds. I also do breathing exercises, and go to the gym regularly. But I have to admit I'm really slack about doing my vocal exercises when I'm not gigging."

You've been through your own real struggles in living with bipolar disorder. You are spreading awareness, reducing the stigma attached

to it and are a great role model for others. What advice would you give to singers with low confidence or singers who suffer from depression?

"I'd advise anyone with low confidence or depression to try Solution Focused Hypnotherapy. It's an amazing combination of psychotherapy and clinical hypnotherapy which boosts your confidence in a very short space of time. In my experience increased confidence lifts depression because then you have the courage to follow your heart and do what it is you really want to do with your life. Solution Focused Hypnotherapy helped me gain the confidence to go from playing to 20 people in a church hall to singing in front of 4,000 people at the Royal Albert Hall."

I've sometimes said to Music students and clients to try to observe and write about their dark times in their songs. 'Dark nights of the Soul' is a book by Thomas Moore which talks about honouring these times rather than resisting them and using it as something positive to enrich you. What's your take on this?

"I practice Tibetan Buddhism and a big part of the Buddhist path is learning mind-training techniques so that you can transform difficult situations into positive experiences. This has helped me hugely in my life, especially living with bipolar disorder. If I hadn't experienced suffering myself I wouldn't be able to write about it in my songs and use my writing to empathise with the suffering of other people.

So that's something really positive that has come out of my own 'dark nights of the soul'. You can always find a silver lining to the cloud, but you can't have that silver lining unless you have the cloud as well. It's so important to learn how to relax and be gentle with yourself when times are tough – to just be with it rather than always trying to resist or run away. One of my favourite proverbs is a Hindu saying: "If you don't worry about a misfortune for three years it will become a blessing."

What stimulates your creativity?

"I see creativity as a reservoir that needs filling up from time to time, so when I get writer's block, I go to art galleries and read lots of poetry to feed my mind. Listening to new music is also a great way of getting inspired again. But at the end of the day it's all about effort, patience and perseverance. As the author Ken Follett says 'The art of writing is the application of the seat of your pants to the seat of the chair.' Or as someone else said, it's 1% Inspiration and 99% Perspiration.'"

Can you define 'Soul?' What is 'Soul' to you?

"I'm a Buddhist so I don't believe in the traditional idea of 'soul' as in the permanent, autonomous essence of a person. I believe in consciousness – the timeless, ever-changing, all-powerful energy of mind. As the song goes, 'I'm a million different people from one day to the next'."

The Music Industry can be a roller coaster. Do you have any philosophies or beliefs that play a part in keeping you positive?

"My Buddhist meditation practice at the beginning and end of each day is an incredibly important part of my life and it helps me through the ups and downs of life in the music business. I try to be philosophical about the low points and grateful for the good bits. And I hold firm to my intention which is to be of some benefit to others through my music. Otherwise I might as well have trained to be an accountant."

Is gratitude important?

"I think gratitude is an essential part of developing a healthy, positive state of mind, of being able to really enjoy your life. We can all find reasons to worry but it's much better to focus on reasons to be happy and be thankful for them. If you can develop this kind of attitude, life will be kind to you. So gratitude is really important but confidence is the key to being successful in what you do. I don't mean success in terms of fame or fortune, but success in terms of achieving your goals and fulfilling your intentions, whatever they are. The main thing is to believe wholeheartedly in what you're doing. As a performer, an audience will recognise that and respond to it.

Because your state of mind is reflected in your voice - If you're feeling timid and anxious, your throat and chest become tight and constricted and that's obvious when you sing. But if you're feeling brave and open and passionate about what you're doing, then people will hear that too. Your whole body – your posture, the expression on your face, your level of energy – changes depending on how you feel, and that affects your performance. And how you feel depends on the thoughts you put in your head, and that's why positive thinking – thoughts that generate love and confidence in your heart - is so important in performing, as it is in life in general."

Deepest thanks to Emily for such a frank and revealing interview. You can check out her music at emilymaguire.com.

Chapter Three

Confidence

True self-confidence is earned through persistence, hard work and experience so it's important to recognise that you're doing the best you can right now in line with your experiences to date.

Try not to envy somebody who you see as more confident than you. Try to simply recognise that they're in a different state to you right now and observe how they act. Learn from them. Many performers are not confident 24/7 and many are able to project confidence in the same way that an actor plays a part. They adopt an on-stage persona to some degree. This may really work for you for a while. So you can 'act-as-if' until you feel truly confident. Many successful singers use a persona for confidence or simply for entertainment as part of their performance and this can take some of the pressure off while you're discovering your own true personal confidence.

True personal confidence is developed from taking risks and breaking through comfort zones. Your learning and performing experiences will also feed your confidence.

Dealing with fear

It often seems that the arch-enemy of a Singer or performer is 'fear' itself. It's really more about your relationship with fear and how you hold the fear so it's different for everyone. So right now I'd like you to consider the following truth that will change your relationship with fear.

***'The fear will never go away as long as you continue to grow.'* - Susan Jeffers**

PAIN  POWER

This means that fear is not a problem but simply part of the process. Whenever you experience a new task, situation or environment you will hear your internal negative 'self-talk,'from your sub-conscious mind telling you to protect yourself which initiates the fear. You don't need to deny the fear. Honour it and push through it. You simply need to push through it by... Doing it anyway! Doing it in spite of fear.

This is the basis of Susan Jeffer's excellent book 'Feel the Fear and do it anyway' where she describes how you can transform fear and indecision into action, or from pain to power. You can break through this fear though and you can do it every time. You can do this with courage and focusing on a positive outcome. Visualise it.

What is the successful result you desire? How does it look, sound, feel? This will increase your expectation for a successful result and in turn reduce your fear. So have great expectations and you will surprise yourself!

Let's be clear on this – Fear is a defensive position created by your ego to protect you. The problem is that this 'protection' doesn't make room for you to break out of fear-based limiting beliefs and doesn't enable you to grow. So one option is to face the fear head on and break through any fear barriers to reveal your inner power and confidence. But don't resist fear. It's not your enemy. Think of fear as a part of your process of becoming a more confident Singer.

Each time you experience fear by trying something new and push through that fear, you break out of your comfort zone and gain another notch of raw confidence in yourself and your ability.

Then a new, wider boundary of confidence appears as your new comfort zone. Each time you anchor in courage to break out of a new comfort zone you INCREASE your personal power as a singer. Also, each time others witness this change in you, you will find even greater encouragement and confidence in your own performance.

Fear-busting techniques for Singers

So let's spell them out and then commit to them.

1. Rehearsing regularly.

2. Warming-up.

3. Letting go.

Rehearsal

When you rehearse a song well, when you've rehearsed it enough you find it becomes a part of you and you 'own it,' the idea of fear is gone because the song feels like 'home' and fear doesn't live there. So rehearse, rehearse, rehearse. Do it for peace of mind and do it because it's fun anyway. It's music after all.

Celebrated artiste, Prince was asked in an interview how he was able to perform as he did. His answer was one word - "Practice."

Anyone who has been fortunate enough to witness a Prince concert performance (and I'm one of them) will tell you that they walked away knowing that they'd just witnessed the greatest show on earth. So 'practice' must be important.

Plan your rehearsal time. Make a short list of what you want to achieve and keep to the plan during rehearsal. Then re-run through anything that needs more work. You're likely to achieve much more and this will greatly boost your confidence.

Warm-up

Warming up your voice is vital for a singer and there are good examples within the 'Body' section of this book. Your voice is a muscle or to be more precise, it's a series of muscles and in the same way that an athlete needs to warm-up their muscles before they perform to avoid muscle strain the same applies to singing.

The basic idea of a vocal warm-up is to get blood to your vocal cords and supporting muscles in a gradual and gentle way so as to avoid any unnecessary strain to your voice when rehearsing or performing.

A vocal warm-up can be designed especially for a singer and tailored for their personal needs. The most effective vocal warm-up which we'll be sharing later is called a 'lip roll' and is the best way to warm your voice devoid of excess tension.

Vocal warm-up's play a great role in lifting your confidence in your voice physically and have a calming effect on you mentally before you perform.

The role of a warm-up is purely to prepare your voice for it's actual workout session, rehearsal or performance so shouldn't be too strenuous. The value of a warm-up in preparing your tone and flexibility can't be overstated and the simple act of you warming up as a routine will enable you stamina and longevity in your singing.

Letting go

This final fear-busting technique needs more attention but gives you a more relaxed focus.

In Barry Green and W, Timothy Gallwey's book 'The Inner game of Music' The concept of "Self 1 and Self 2" lays the foundation for most discussions: Every musician involves two "self aspects" in terms of their performance - Self 1 is logical, judgmental, and self-conscious, Self 2 is spontaneous, natural. We should apply techniques to be more aware about Self 2. Our goal is to let Self 2 express the most, and re-frame the impact of Self 1.

Another concept reveals three aspects of training - will, trust, and awareness.

You can increase will power by setting clear goals. You can develop trust in yourself by developing confidence and focus. You can also develop greater awareness or mindfulness by connecting with emotions and memories that you can use to expressively fuel your performance.

For example, you can 'let go' of the need to be perfect by creatively 'letting go to randomness.' This means you lean towards random, experimental or more improvisational singing instead of simply following a set melody - as heard in some forms of Jazz.

You can 'let go' of the need to impress an audience by 'letting go to the music' In this way you focus only on the feeling of the music and the words completely and let the words and music consume you as though you're experiencing and delivering them for the first time till nothing else is engaged. Only the music remains.

When you focus on the real reason you sing or play music--for enjoyment, self expression and authentic expression of the human spirit... If this then becomes the focus, all of the rest will fall in place.

Self-Esteem

Self – esteem is also a contributor to the mindset of a performer and low self-esteem can render you almost paralysed on stage. If you have low self-esteem you may have a limiting belief that relates to feeling low self-worth or that you're 'not enough.'

Self-esteem is affected by how we view ourselves foremost and this can make you more sensitive to others opinions of you which further trigger or re-inforces your negative belief. Some people keep working on goals and things that help them feel good about themselves to keep their focus positive but in your subconscious the belief is still there so you can find yourself constantly working without relief.

The bottom line though and one that MANY overlook because of subconscious limiting beliefs, social programming and the media... is the importance of self-love.

Self-love is NOT self-ish. It's not the same thing at all. You are born worthy of love and respect. Events or experiences can obscure that truth and if you recognise this with yourself you need to focus on all of the positive things about yourself and begin to accept yourself AS YOU ARE. This is the basis of self-love and creates the healthy roots of good self-steem.

Your giving to others, your contribution to society... in fact all of these things can be fake and pointless if you don't actually have love and respect for yourself.

What I mean here is truly accepting and approving of yourself 100% and being grateful for everything about yourself. For some of us, let's face it, this doesn't sound so easy and depending on your past and present experiences in life it might feel a strange concept. The truth is that the people who truly practice self-love have self-respect and a greater capacity to give to others and all of their goals in life have greater passion simply because they started with the primary goal of honouring themselves and their own feelings first. Not to the detriment of others feelings though but in a healthy way.

Self-love is knowing yourself, having healthy boundaries and knowing yourself well enough to honour what you want and how you feel. When you think about it low self-worth is endemic in the world and causes much suffering. I'd like to share with you a simple process that you can use if you struggle with self-worth and here's the truth... Almost everybody does at some time so you're not alone.

Each day or in any situation ask yourself "What would somebody who loved themself do?" Your answer to this question will be a self-loving one and making a habit of this will enable you to build your self-worth and self-esteem.

For some it takes more dedication to realise you are a human being that is worthy of respect and love. No matter what. If you have low self-esteem this is not your fault and may be the result of your own personal experiences or unconscious feelings from your childhood. That's not to blame anyone else. Just recognise it, acknowledge it, let it go and let's focus on moving on to the new you. Many people have low self-esteem issues in an industry which sometimes obsesses over it's marketing a warped idea of 'perfection.' The music industry increasingly demands high levels of confidence and self-belief. If self-esteem is an issue for you please know that you're not alone and you can make building your own self-esteem a daily habit by focusing simply on only doing the things that make you feel good, without judgement. Teal Swan has made a series of youtube videos which address low self esteem and you will benefit from her understanding. She also offers a number of processes to move forward on her website.

Simply the act of singing is a great therapeutic release, releasing endorphines and is very good for you. Be assured that as you develop your vocal ability and begin to perform regularly your self -esteem will skyrocket. Fear is self-created and starts in the mind. As a singer this may begin as self-conscious worry about what 'they' think – Your audience, friends, family … in fact anybody who might possibly give you a nega-tive or indifferent reaction and perhaps shoot down your efforts, hopes and dreams. Develop trust that ANY audience is your cheering squad and wants you to have faith in yourself.

Actively seek situations that will provide you with opportunities to build your self-esteem. This is usually doing anything which makes you feel good about being yourself. There are also a number of books which specialise in this area.

Dealing with Limiting Beliefs

Beliefs affect our view of the world and there are some beliefs which we form or are conditioned during our childhood which are unhealthy to our development and ultimately our happiness and these are called limiting beliefs.

These beliefs are often formed during our childhood but often are conditioned by society or our social structures and the belief forms in our sub-conscious mind as a kind of programming.

Consider any beliefs you hold which are limiting you or holding you back from achieving your full potential because once you are aware of them you can change them or replace them with beliefs which serve you.

This is especially crucial if the belief is holding you back in your singing and from growing self-confidence.

The Silva method, Self-hypnosis, Cognitive Behavioural Therapy and NLP (Neuro-Linguistic Programming) are each great methods that can teach you to uproot and replace limiting beliefs that might either block or limit your progress in anything you seek to do.

Here are some examples of limiting beliefs and their counter belief.

Limiting Belief - What if I'm too old?

Counter Belief - There is NO age limit with singing, I get better and better and my singing expresses my greater experience. You don't stop singing because you grow old. You grow old because you stop singing.

Limiting Belief - I have a poor vocal range

Counter Belief - I know my comfortable range and I can employ techniques and a coach to expand my range. My range is adequate and I have unlimited potential.

TASK

Be honest with yourself and make a list of any limiting beliefs or negative thoughts that you consider about your own singing.

You might have to consider if a negative is actually covering up a limiting belief. Ask yourself in what way is this negative statement REALLY 100% true?

For each Limiting belief, Write a counter belief and state it out loud. It might surprise you as you do this how you begin to feel lighter and it may even surprise you that you had such negative beliefs. The main thing is that now that you've gained full awareness of them and realise that they are not serving you, you can replace them with ones that serve you. YOU are the creator of your life and no longer permit your sub-conscious or social programming to rule the show. Realising this places the power in your hands.

For best and lasting effect, write out your counter beliefs and each day state them as affirmations. This commits you to the new belief which serves much better and constant repetition is what's needed to replace the limiting belief in your subconsious mind.

Lee Risdale

Affirmations

Scientists now agree that our sub-conscious mind runs 90% of the show. It seems more and more obvious that our sub-conscious mind rules us more than WE do so we need to be very mindful of what's in there and what we plant there. Anyone who's seen the Hollywood movie, Inception might know what I mean.

So let's replace any limiting beliefs with positive self-serving ones that will sky-rocket you towards achieving your singing goals and your life goals. This is where affirmations come into play. An affirmation is a positive statement you make to yourself. Constant spaced repetition of an affirmation enables you to plant a new belief in your subconscious.

A more direct route, though is by planting the counter belief or affirmation in your subconscious during meditation at Alpha level and this is easier to do than you might think if you're persistent (See meditation using The Silva Method as discussed earlier).

When you write out your own affirmations, make sure you write them in the present tense and write them in a way that is personally believable enough for you without inflating your ego into complete delusion.

If you write 'I am the greatest singer in the world,' yet there is no evidence of that (yet) you might have a hard time getting that one to take for you. Your subconscious won't accept it and this kind of self deceit will feel fake. Here are some examples of good ones but please judge for yourself what feels acceptable for you and write your own.

I am a good enough singer (you can replace 'good enough' with 'good' or 'great' etc.)
My singing is getting better and better everyday
I always give my best and that is good enough for right now
I love singing/performing and I express my passion
I sing for myself and share with the audience
If I enjoy it the audience enjoys it
I am a master

Of course your mindset and use of affirmations isn't everything because there is action and effort that must follow to achieve your goal of becoming the best singer you can be. But creating this mindset is vital because it plants the seeds that everything else follows from. Don't be surprised if when you develop a more positive and clear mindset towards your singing and performing (banishing any negative self-talk) that everything else seems to come together for you more quickly - Just as if you are a magnet. It's because you've programmed yourself for success. You've set the stage.

As mentioned in Chapter two when we talked about focus - Another very useful technique to get you in a great mindset for singing or performing is to banish any thoughts of the past or future and simply focus only on the present moment. In 'the NOW' time stands still and the only thing that's important is enjoying the present moment and making the most of each second you're singing. Forget everything else and focus only on the act of what you're singing in the moment. This is pure creativity and pure expression, clear of any limiting thoughts or damaging self-talk. The NOW is the only thing that really exists. When you think about it that's the only thing that matters.

Do you always feel most alive when you're singing and do you find that everything else that might have happened in the past or might happen in the future doesn't matter in that moment? The 'NOW' is all there is and it feels SO GOOD. This is the basis of the artful practice of mindfulness.

From observing Professional Singers we find a balance of each in these areas:

1. A passion for singing which inspires vocal work on a daily basis. This creates consistency.

2. Curiosity and research of the recordings of great singers in history.

3. Ability to achieve emotional calm or focus in order to concentrate.

4. Healthy physical exercise and understanding that the voice and the rest of the body are connected.

5. Study for development and moving forward constantly in the learning process.

6. Meditation or some form of relaxation technique.

7. Body work; massage, Alexander technique, shiatsu, yoga, dancing or another body discipline that encourages fitness and body awareness.

8. Appropriate amount of rest; 8 hours Sleep recommended each night.

9. Desire to help other singers in their quest. This helps a singer to avoid becoming overly self-focused.

10. Balance between working time and relaxation time.

Practice these mindful techniques and re-read this section whenever you need a boost to fire your motivation. Keeping a great mindset and positive focus is the primary goal and sets you up for developing and integrating the other two sections of this book - Body and Soul... and then integrating them as a complete vocalist's process.

Interview with

Soul Legend

Geno Washington

Lee Risdale

What a night! Geno Washington & The Ram Jam Band were excellent. The audience clapped and cheered long after Geno left the stage following a rapturous encore. One of many that this man has performed in his career spanning over five decades. Geno had achieved a legendary status as a live performer ever since the sixties as he toured the Uk and had a number one LIVE album. The fact that a live album is a number one best seller at any time is telling of the magnetic appeal of Geno Washington. During the eighties *Dexy's Midnight Runners* recorded a number one single written about him called *Geno*. At one time in fact anyone from Jimi Hendrix to The Rolling Stones would be cueing up to see him perform.

I met Geno after the gig and I interviewed him. It struck me how this man, a Soul legend is still sounding so great after over 50 years in the music business.

My meeting with Geno surpassed all my expectations and we got on like a house on fire. I discovered that under his joking, down-to-earth but larger than life personality he is also a very smart and very kind man.

He gave me a lot of his time, answered all of my questions and gave me some excellent advice. He even shared a hypnotist trick with me too.

It was very much like having an intimate conversation with an old friend even though there were several musicians in and out of the Moles Club backstage dressing room which is more like a cupboard under the stairs (Think Harry Potter).

This is high energy music and somebody once told me Soul singers always die young. His vocal range is still fantastic! Later, Geno admitted to me he is seventy years old (!) which prompted me to ask...

Me: "So Geno, what's your secret...?"

Geno: "They die young when they party hard and become addicted to that high. You need to condition your mind to stay in control."

He then looked me right in the eyes and repeated a profound message, he was intent on telling me -

"Change your thoughts and you change your life."

He told me that he meditates every day. Surprising to some, it's not uncommon knowledge that many of the best singers understand the benefits of meditation which has mental and physical benefits that have been measured scientifically (see The Silva Method). I asked him how he goes about it and he explained that the meditation is based on 'self-hypnosis' which I knew that he had studied and qualified in.

I found out he has excellent 'awareness' and doesn't miss a trick, even after large glasses of red wine. He told me that due to his joking personality often people don't expect it but he is a careful listener and soaks up everything like a sponge. I guess you could say that he is 'hyper-aware' and meditation/self-hypnosis seems to have kept his mind sharp. He's sharp alright! The band's set was intelligently thought through. Any musician could tell that. Even with a dep drummer who Geno nick-named 'Handsome Dave' the setlist was slick.

Early in our conversation he addressed me by my name and said "from a singer to a singer" which was really charming. His conversation with his audience is outrageously entertaining and 'on the edge.' He really works the audience and has them singing lines back to him.

Me: "When you first step out on stage, what goes through your mind?"

Geno: "To get the audience."

Me: "You've always had a great way of drawing in your audience. What advice would you give to young singers starting out about stagecraft and how you relate to an audience?"

Geno: "I use 'suggestion' with the audience - Hypnotic language."

He then told me that an under-confident performer would benefit from studying 'self-hypnosis' and we discussed how you can impress the sub-conscious mind with what you want to change your thoughts from fear to confidence.

Geno: "If you really want to be a singer, use self-hypnosis because your conscious mind loves you more than YOU do."

Me: "Can you explain what 'Soul' means to you? Can you define 'Soul?'

Geno: "Soul is singing from deep in your heart and sharing it with the world."

I felt a real affinity with Geno and we had a great conversation, he answered all of my questions and we had some great laughs too. Geno appreciated the purpose of this book and I promised to send him a copy when it's finished. I warmly thanked him for talking with me and said good-bye.

For many reasons it's easy to see why the audience were still chanting 'Geno! Geno!" at the end of the night... as did Dexy's Midnight Runners in all of their performances.

Interview with

Singer and Performance Coach,

Kizzy Morrell

Lee Risdale

Kizzy Morrell has been singing and involved in the Music Business from a young age and had many successes, not least that she is today an inspiring and influential figure as both a Performance Coach for Youth talent is Bristol, England having won a prestigious award in recognition of her work and she also hosts her own radio show in the heart of Bristol at Ujima Radio. I asked her to contribute her mindful and encouraging ideas both as a Singer and Performance coach.

Me: "When you first step out on a stage to sing, what goes through your mind?"

Breathe … because I still get nervous sometimes before I perform so I remember that I can take a good deep breath which helps to relax me, steady my nerves and help and prepare me to sing.

Me: "How do you get 'in the zone' when you perform? Is it all about the songs?"

Yes, I like to sing songs I feel a real connection with so I can really express the meaning. I also like to go somewhere quiet if I can before I perform. Even if for just five minutes. It helps me feel calm and more prepared.

Me: "Do you warm up your voice before you sing?"

I like to use a lip roll as a siren to warm my low and high notes gently without tension.

Me: "Do you have any good remedies for a sore throat?"

Honey, lemon and Ginger in hot water.

Me: "Can you explain what 'Soul' means to you? Can you define 'Soul?'"

It's your spiritual connection and how you express yourself deeply with the music.

Me: "Geno Washington recently said to me "Change your thoughts and you change your life." What's your take on this statement?

Yes, I agree with that. When you have a positive attitude it affects everything you do and people react to that. Also events transpire around you favourably when you have a positive mental attitude. It's a universal law. This is especially important for artistes and performers who needs to be resilient.

Me: "What advice would you give to singers with low confidence or singers who suffer from depression?"

Feel the fear and do it anyway...Keep singing, keep playing gigs and keep putting yourself out there and your comfort zone will expand, as will your confidence.

Me: "The Music Industry can be a roller coaster. Do you have any and advice for singers starting out or making their way from your experience?"

Get a really good manager. Someone you can trust.

Me: "You do great work with your Performance Company 'Studio 7' … What qualities do you like to help develop in the Singers you work with?

Good communication skills are important. Also to have respect for other artistes/musicians. I like encourage them most of all in developing their own style.

Discover more about Kizzy's work at www.kizzymorrell.com, www. studio-7.co.uk, www.regionalyouthmusicawards.com/ and http:// ujimaradio.com

Part Two

THE BODY

"You should practice as much as you perform, even more."
- Seth Riggs (Legendary Vocal Coach to Michael Jackson
and Stevie Wonder)

Wait... So I can get better by training?

It always surprises me... every time. Some people simply think that singers are either born to sing... or not.

It's as if Beyonce was delivered from her mothers womb with microphone in hand singing a Destiny's Child number. 'Yep, she's alway been great, born great... so easy for her.'

Really...? Bet she could tell you a different story.

The opposite of this is also surprising. The idea that your voice is as good as it's ever going to get. It's the 'Ah well, I've just got this range and I just sing these songs. Yeah, my voice can't do that. I'm limited.' This is complete bull.

Not to say that it's helpful to have perspective. If I feel I can't humanly sing a high 'C' that's ok... but does it mean I shouldn't ever aspire to work towards it and extend my range?

I'm here to reassure you right now that often the labels given to vocal ranges and voice types are archaic and have a very limiting place in modern contemporary music. In saying that, by all means, if it does makes you feel good and more comfortable knowing that you're a baritone or a soprano, please enjoy it. Just keep in mind that often these labels or boxes were designed to keep singers with otherwise unlimited potential in a desirable vocal range. It's a 'group singing' design used to balance voices in a choir. Sometimes, a box to confine your potential.

Not only is it possible to extend your vocal range with practice. You can also...

Develop and enhance your tone
Develop greater breath control
Increase your volume/power
Develop greater strength and flexibility

Let's also establish that even GREAT singers had to work at it. They need to keep working at it, too... even moreso to meet the demands of their profession and a demanding Music Industry.

The Importance of Training your Body

Ok, so now we're getting into an exciting part of this book. The flesh and bones. The meat and potatoes (in an attempt to include meat-eaters or vegetarians... but eat more veggies singers!).

I'm presenting the case for the importance of attention to Mind, Body and Soul in your singing. Your voice is a physical instrument and you carry it with you at all times. You can strengthen it and make it more flexible with exercise and practice. Exercising your voice is important.

Before we begin it's worth mentioning that you can have a really expressive voice and cleverly adapt your own style to cover up imperfections in your physical vocal technique. You might say these Singers use Mind and Soul, yet they're constantly covering up their weakness. It's said that there are a select few Singers who are born lucky into having a voice which requires very little work or development, if any. This is very rare though and most of us mere mortals have to work at it... like anything. Like anything that's worth working at, your voice is well and truly worth it. If you love singing, you won't mind exercising your voice. Exercises might not be as exciting or fulfilling as singing songs but it's sooo important and ultimately hugely rewarding.

You may have heard of the Chinese martial art known as Kung Fu. Although you might be familiar with the term Kung Fu made famous by great pioneers such as Bruce Lee you might be interested to learn what the term actually means. Kung Fu means 'continual hard work' and can relate to any discipline. So you see, Singing can also be Kung Fu when you have the intention to always be developing and improving your ability. There is always more to learn in any discipline and there is no end to what you can develop.

It's best to think of your voice as a physical muscle that needs to be exercised in a number of ways. It needs to be exercised regularly too to be at it's best. To be more specific your voice is a complex series of muscles and supporting muscles that when working together efficiently are capable of achieving notes and phrases of such power and flexibility that are nothing short of athletic.

In this chapter you'll be learning many tools and exercises that are the key to building and developing your physical voice from the bottom upwards. This means we'll cover posture, breathing, tone-building, support muscles and demonstrate various techniques that can greatly contribute to your singing and energise you with a full tool-box of techniques you can work with.

In each area I'll be sharing tasks, exercises and techniques for you to try and with repetition and persistence you'll discover how they will gradually transform your singing. Ok, are you ready....? Then let's get started. Exercising and taking care of your voice will ensure you get to keep it strong and healthy for a long time. If you neglect to sing regularly or practice the opposite may show itself to you without warning. This can reveal itself as poor breath control, vocal fatigue, strain, soreness, hoarseness, swollen cords or at worst - nodules and polyps. So, it will help you to keep a regular warm-up and vocal exercise routine that maximises your vocal ability and keeps your voice balanced and consistent to meet the demands of regular and improved singing.

Chapter One

Posture

At some point in your life you may have received some advice from others on posture...But what is good posture for a singer?

Poor posture puts strain on muscles or de-activates others. The action of this is that some muscles can become too tight or interfere with the process of singing. So, when muscles that are not needed get involved they can only have a detrimental or straining effect. This might not always be obvious but it will wear on your voice over time and cause you difficulty until you find you need to seek professional help, voice therapy or at worse case, an operation to repair damage to your vocal cords.

There is a natural curve in your lower spine and changes to this are the root of posture problems. When standing or walking try to keep your abs slightly flexed, your shoulders back and your head balanced high on your shoulders, as if a string is holding it up.

Common problems can occur if your back is either flat or too arched. This forces other muscles to contract and put you off balance. Balance is vital to singing and if you are not grounded with both feet planted firmly on the floor you will mis-place tension in the wrong muscles. I challenge you to try singing whilst standing on one leg and you'll understand what I mean.

Holding your shoulders up too tightly will cause unwanted tension that creeps it's way to the surrounding muscles of your larynx. Your larynx houses your vocal cords which make your tone and any undue tension here can cause tightness of related muscles. So, this can affect how you sing.

Here is a checklist to remember;

1. Keep your feet grounded.

2. Natural curve of your lower back.

3. Abdominals mildly flexed.

4. Shoulders back, yet relaxed.

5. Head, tilted slightly upwards.

Three basic principals of good posture are verticality, stability and muscle/joint balance. In his book, The Musician's Body, Dr. Jaume Rosset I Lobet explains these principals and I'll summarise them for you here.

Verticality is about making the most of your height. Try to imagine a vertical line passing down from the top of your head through the centre of your body. You can check your posture in a full length mirror. Ask yourself... Am I standing symetrically from left to right? How are my shoulders? Too high, tensed? Hunched? Relaxed? How am I holding my head? Does it poke forward or upwards? This can bring in unwanted muscles and sometimes cut of some of your airflow. Does it sit in line with my shoulders?

Stability is firstly about being properly grounded with both feet firmly planted and slightly apart for good balance. Distribute your weight evenly throughout the soles of your feet, ball to heel. Keep your knees slightly bent and 'rock your pelvis,' (excuse the phrase Elvis fans). Rock your pelvis slightly forward as this helps maintain the natural curve of your spine.

Muscle and Joint Balance can be affected as we grow older or if we don't exercise because your abdominal muscles can become weaker and the muscles at back of your thighs become shorter and more tense, less flexible.

This affects your posture. You can counteract this by toning these muscles which provide invaluable support for a singers posture.

Stretch the muscles at the back of your leg for 20 seconds. Next, raise your leg with knee bent and push against it with your hand. Apply equal resistance so that neither hand or legs wins. Apply this 10 times for each leg.

Try checking your posture in a full length mirror.

1. Imagine a vertical line passing through each ear, shoulder, hip and ankle.

2. Keep your head upright and vertical, imagine it being suspended by a string above your shoulders.

3. Keep your shoulders relaxed. Don't tense or raise your shoulders.

4. Keep your ribs lifted, allowing more freedom for breathing; avoid hunching.

5. Pelvis slightly tilted forward to reduce strain on spine.

6.   Avoid exaggerating spinal curve; don't lean back too far.

7.   Knees slightly bent, soft – without tensing your legs.

8.   Keep your feet slightly apart, firmly on the floor for balance and equal body-weight distribution between each leg. Equally distribute between the ball and heel of each foot.

If you can keep these in your awareness when singing it will make a long-term and worthwhile difference to both your singing and your confidence. A confident person walks this way and a confident singer performs this way.

Keep this in mind when you're standing and when you walk, step from the hip and swing your arms in flowing motion. Doing this as a habit can improve both your posture and your confidence in time. It can take a while, sometime months of repetition for a new postural habit to take a permanent effect so awareness and persistence are the keys to success in adopting good posture with your singing.

If you are sitting while singing it's common for some singers to slightly hunch. This is because a flat-based chair makes your pelvis rock backwards and you lose the natural lumbar curve of your spine. This new inverted curve of your lower spine tenses your diaphragm and restricts your breathing. So, sitting up is important and the best thing to do is to sit on the front edge of the chair, giving better positioning of your pelvis, natural lumbar curve and your entire back. You can also work on your Core body strength with this excellent exercise to develop your abdominal support. Lie face down on the floor. Use our forearms with palms facing upwards, down to your elbows to lift and support your body. Flex your abs and keep your back straight. Now hold this position for a count of 20. Repeat this four times.

Understanding these principals can improve your awareness of your posture but by making it a habit with repetition will improve and instil a great posture for your singing.

If you can take up another regular exercise that you enjoy this will help. Running is one of the quickest ways to strengthen you whilst making you more limber and flexible. It has the added bonus of helping you lose weight very quickly and improve your breath control. I took up running on a whim and it made a big difference to my health and my singing. Swimming, aerobics, pilates or Yoga are just some of the pursuits that have great health benefits and will each go some way to improving your posture. If you choose weight training I recommend picking something else as well that enables you to keep your muscles flexible but not too tight, such as dancing.

Many styles of dancing help you to develop a good posture that will enhance your singing. I got into Northern Soul dancing as a natural part of singing Soul music and I quickly found that it made a dramatic impact on my posture, my health and my energy levels. It feels fantastic to do as well.

Maybe you could consider learning a dance style that fits your favourite style of music and incorporate that in your own performance. It's great fun and beats going to the gym or any other disciplined exercise regime hands down in my opinion. Besides, why would you suffer tedious exercise in the pursuit of health when you can dance?

If you're gigging regularly though you might find that rocking out onstage might be all the exercise you need but keep aware of your onstage posture, especially if you play an instrument.

Breath Control

Why is breath control important?

To support your voice you need to create a solid base to control the sound and although this can appear straight forward to do, it can require regular practice and rehearsal to do well.

Here's the process. As you breath in (inhale) your diaphragm drops down allowing your lungs to fill with air and expand. This is your diaphragm muscle's natural reflex and it happens subconsciously when you sleep.

It's second reflex is to relax back to it's original position, moving back up and this is what gently squeezes the air out of the lungs.

Your main job within this process when singing is to ensure your breath is LOW in the body so you can control the air on the outbreath. This control is what you need to sustain a note or phrase for longer than just a few seconds.

Using abdominal muscles and the intercostal muscles between your ribs assists your diaphragm in doing this for maximum support. Another muscle of support is the pelvic diaphragm or pelvic floor and this can create additional lower intra-abdominal pressure and support using perennials, levator ani, and coccygeus muscles. How this 'feels' as an action is a feeling of 'leaning outwards' with your abs and a feeling of expansion in your lower ribcage. Pelvic muscles 'pull in.' This combination creates ultimate breath support.

Diaphragmatic Breathing

You may have heard people often talking about diaphragmatic breathing as though it's some unearthly Jedi skill that needs to be mastered.

Diaphragmatic breathing is actually very natural. It's good to lie on your back to really experience it. Here's a simple exercise you can try and it'll help you to really feel what's happening.

Take a book. Lie on your back on the floor and place the book on your stomach. Take ten deep breaths into your abdomen and as you do notice the book rising and falling. Anchor in this feeling of allowing your breath to drop low down into your body with your stomach relaxed to allow it to expand. This is diaphragmatic breathing.

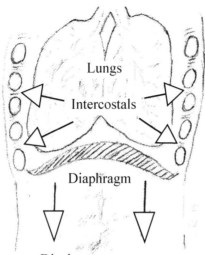

Lungs

Intercostals

Diaphragm

Diaphragm contracts
and flattens

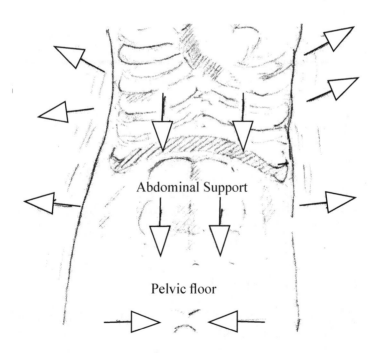

Abdominal Support

Pelvic floor

Here are some breathing techniques to practice and enable you to get a better sense of your deep breathing.

Exercise 1 – (360 Degree Technique)

360 Degree Breath Technique will... Encourage more outward movement and control using supported muscles (Abdominal muscle breathing instead of upper body breathing).

Helps you...Relax your throat, reduce nasality of tone, blend your registers, Improve resonance, reduce chance of any vocal damage and increase your vocal range.

1) Low breath into stomach awareness - Place your hand on your stomach. Take a breath and notice that as you inhale the air is you are inhaling is pushing your stomach out against your hand. As you exhale your stomach moves back inwards as your breath is released. Do this 5-10 times and observe this movement.

2) Low breath into lower back awareness - Place your palms in the back (in the kidney area). Hunch over slightly as your do this to really observe the movement. Push your palms into your back slightly. Inhale a deep breath and notice the lower back pushing outwards. Then release. Do this 5-10 times to get a real sense of breathing into the lower back.

3) Low breath into ribcage (Intercostal muscles). Place fingertips on the sides of your ribs and inhale to breath the ribcage outwards. Then release. Do this 10 times to get a real feeling of your ribcage expanding. Diaphragm is connected to the ribcage and this is great support for it. Keep your lower ribs 'high & wide' to help fully sustain and support a note.

Exercise 2 – Depth Perception

Depth perception (related to Basketball/netball practice) Breath Perception : Points of reference by Practice.

Practice 'eee' on 5 tone scale in this progression. 1) One set 2) Three 2) Three Sets 3) Six Sets

You need about one scale worth of air to spare (at least) so you hold pitch till the end comfortably.

Exercise 3 - Breath Control for High Notes

It's in the way you set it up. If you set it up wrong, the sustain will continue incorrectly (wobbly, pitchy etc).

1)   Keep your airflow consistent and don't spend your air too fast.

2)   Keep Compression consistent. Vocal compression is the degree of vocal cord closure or resistance to the airflow that we make by adducting our with our vocal folds. Using stomach & pelvic muscles and leaning outwards with your abdominal muscles and downwards pelvic floor pressure, sing Na na na na on an Octave Repeater exercises. As you engage pelvic floor/diaphragm muscles while sitting down, practice maintaining the same consistent level of tone... whilst increasing airflow.

Now that you have the basics and have practiced these exercises we can simplify the process. If you're always wondering 'am I breathing correctly?' then your body can get confused and breathing will be inconsistent.

So simply commit to taking a LOW BREATH and supporting that breath well as you exhale. This means don't spend your air too quickly and just make sure you don't stack up too much breath, remembering to breath out too. Use your instincts to measure how much breath you need for a phrase and you will improve this with practice. It can help to make some breath marks on your lyric sheet as a guide when you're working on a song that's new to you.

Lee Risdale

Appoggio Technique

Appoggio technique comes from Italian Bel Canto. It is Italian for 'support' and derives from Appoggiare with means 'to lean upon.'

The principle of Appoggio is that in keeping your sternum (middle of lower ribcage) elevated, held high, you can reduce or better control the rate of sub-glottal pressure when you release your breath and tone.

You can experience this ideal elevated sternum posture by raising both arms above your head. Your sternum naturally rises when your arms are in this position - suspending, but not holding, the breath with the inspiration muscles. Then try lowering your arms while exhaling slowing without lowering your sternum.

When done well this breath retention can minimise subglottic pressure or the rate of breath exhalation. When we inhale, subglottic pressure is at its lowest level and lung volume at its highest. Staying in the position of initial inhalation gives a singer the sensation of 'singing on the posture of inhalation.' Although we don't inhale as we sing, we are simply making the gesture, or keeping the same posture - instead of that of exhalation. There is more control available when sustaining notes in this position.

Here is another way to describe Appoggio which can be related to riding a bicycle. Imagine riding a bicycle down a hill and using a brake as your speed control.

Bike speed = Airflow speed

Gravity = Low abdominal support

Brake = Diaphragm

Your brake (diaphragm) is balancing your control of speed (airflow) and therefore by it's steady engagement, enables a smooth descent (steady pitch.)

So Appoggio describes a posture:

1) Keep your sternum raised (keep lower ribcage high and wide). Think of a Lion or Lioness walking majestically.

2) This creates a vaccuum of air. Air expanded into ribcage, expansion of your lower back and the front of your torso which allows your lungs to fully inflate.

3) Maintain this same posture during your exhalation. Pull down and outwards with your abdominal muscles and diaphragm.

4) Resist the collapse of your ribcage using your intercostal muscles between your ribs and your abdominals. This will feel like 'leaning outwards'with these muscles to maintain the posture. Your stretched intercostals, abdominals gluts and pelvic floor all assist in a stack-up to support your diaphragm.

I sometimes find it useful to ask my students to visualise a spinning tornado inside their ribcage, keeping the ribcage open for ultimate support, taking care to relax the shoulders.

Your diaphragm is shaped much like a parachute when it is relaxed and when you breath in to receive air into your lungs, it flattens downwards like a trampoline.

Exercise

To fully experience your diaphragm at work:

1) Bend over like a rag doll.

2) Breath deeply and with your hands, feel just below your sterum and lower rib-cage.

3) Notice your diaphragm expanding (engaging) and contracting (relaxing).

Lee Risdale

Tone

Tone is the sound and timbre of a voice. The sound can be thin, fat, round, breathy or wispy, full, raspy... just to name a few descriptions that have been used for tone.

Tone is made by the vibration of your vocal cords and the anatomical term is vocal folds. Vocal cords are often misspelled as 'vocal chords' but they are not actually cords or strings as often believed.

Vocal cords are skin-like flaps made of mucous membrane and muscle stretched across the opening of the throat or trachea. They form a 'V' shape with the narrow end at the front of the larynx and opening from the back.

Male and female vocal cords usually differ in size, around 17-25mmm in length in men and 12.5 - 17.5mm in women. This in part, as well as larynx size and other factors accounts for the difference in vocal range between men and women.

When we are breathing the vocal cords are in a relaxed or open state which is sometimes described as 'abducted.' When we talk, cough or swallow they 'adduct' or come together.

Air from the lungs creates sub-glottal pressure which cause the vocal cords to oscillate. When they are pushed apart by this airflow, the cords natural resilience brings them back together. This process is called a 'vibratory cycle.'

To create a given pitch the cords have to oscillate at a relevant speed and frequency. This opening and closing (oscillation) to hundreds of times per second is what creates tone and pitch.

The longer that the vocal cords are in the closed phase the more body of tone can be created.

Cord Closure

A 'breathy' sounding voice happens when the cord are positioned in a way that allows more air to leak between them. When singing in Falsetto there is an oval space left between the cords through which more air escapes and the effect is a very light tone. The air escape increases as this space widens with an increase of airflow.

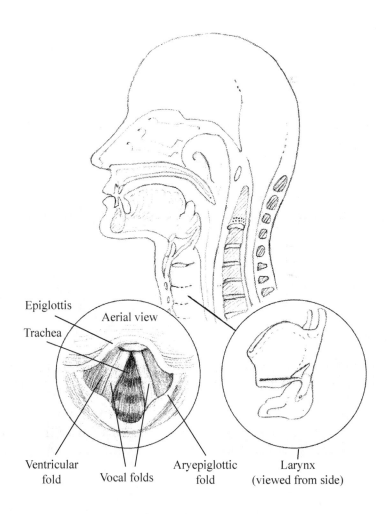

Epiglottis

Trachea

Aerial view

Ventricular fold

Vocal folds

Aryepiglottic fold

Larynx (viewed from side)

A 'pressed' sounding or 'over-compressed' sound happens when the vocal cords are pressed together more than is necessary and this can produce an intense yet slightly forced production of tone. Too much of this can lose vocal power and overuse can damage the vocal folds.

So when we consider these two extremes it becomes clear that a balance is needed and that's why the most efficiently produced vocal sound is made by a small separation of vocal cords which enables the best vibration to be made.

So, simplified:

Poor cord closure = Breathy tone
Excessive cord closure = Over-compressed tone
Good cord closure = Balanced tone

"Volume is the direct result of the vocal cords ability to resist air pressure" - Seth Riggs (Speech Level Singing pioneer)

So here are some exercises to develop your tone and create a balanced consistent cord closure or cord adduction. It's all about balance so what you're aiming for here is a smooth, consistent sound and a clear body of tone. The nature of the exercises will encourage this naturally but what you're moving away from is 'breathy' or 'pressed' which equates to 'breathy = too much air in the sound' or 'pressed = tightness in the sound.'

Exercise One: Working on tone

1) Make a hum on a 'Mm' consonant. You can sing on a five tone scale or major scale or hum to any song you're familiar with but begin lower in your range.

2) Next, using the hum make the sound you'd make when tasting some delicious food. 'Mmmmmm!!!'

3) Using this enthusiastic edgy 'Mmm' continue singing on the scales or melody.

Exercise Two: Working on tone

1) Say the word 'sing.'

2) Next sing only using the 'ng' part of the word. Notice your tongue position up at the back, touching your hard palate. You can sing on a five tone scale or major scale or hum to any song you're familiar with but begin lower in your range.

3) Keeping the 'ng' sound and tongue position sing on a major scale or melody.

Closing the false folds causes constriction and cuts off the airflow dramatically as well as the tone. Here are some kinaesthetic cues for you to retract or release constriction of the false folds:-

1) Yawn.

2) Sing 'Ah' on a five tone scale.

3) Sing 'Oo' to 'Aa' repeatedly focuses on the feeling of the 'AA' vowell.

4) Sing 'Oo' or 'Aa' as a Siren starting low in range up to as high as comfortable up to an octave then back down.

Lifting the Soft Palate

Your soft palette is the fleshy tissue just behind your hard palette which is the roof of your mouth. To enable you to feel your soft palette first use the tip of your tongue to feel the roof of your mouth (the hard palette) and then roll your tongue backwards till you feel the softer tissue at the top/back of your mouth. This is the soft palette and you have control over whether lift it up or leave it in it's lower rested position.

The position you use your soft palate in speech by personal habit alters the acoustic of your voice so that when your soft palate is in a low position you get more nasal resonance and less aural and chest resonance. When you lift your soft palate as you un-hinge your jaw and relax your tongue you get a fuller body of sound which includes a mix of chest and mouth resonance simply because you've made more space for these sound vibrations to occur.

If your soft palate is low by habit your voice can sound very nasal because it makes less space is in the mouth, forcing the sound vibrations to occur more so in the resonance space of the nasal cavity behind your nose. This creates the effect of a bright, thinner yet distinctive sound that we sometimes describe as nasal. This isn't necessarily a bad thing and the nasal cavity is an important component in mixing or mix voice but when lifting your soft palette you're essentially mixing more bass and mid-range into your sound which creates a full sounding and broader range of frequencies. Here is a useful way to think of it as an EQ but when singing you're often using varying levels of all three.

Chest = Bass to Mid-range
Mouth = Mid-range to Treble
Head/Nasal cavity = Treble

Here's an exercise which promotes lifting your soft palette and so you can experiment with how if feels and sounds.

Sing an Italian sounding 'Ah' on a five tone scale. Begin low in your range and work up into your upper register (Think 'Mama mia'). Bridges of the voice require narrowing of the vowell (see vowell modification) for best technique with this exercise though. Also try alternating between 'Ah' and 'Uh' and 'Ah' and 'Oo' singing single notes and then between two notes that are a fourth or fifth interval apart.

Singing 'Ungh' to 'Ah' also works really well to exercise your soft palate and encourage lean muscle and tissue.

Pharyngeal muscles

Pharyngeal muscles are located at the back inside wall of your pharynx. These flexible muscles relax and contract. When you contract or tighten your pharyngeal muscles they effect is to add a brighter, brassy, metallic band of frequencies to your tone which is sometimes described as 'twang.'

This brassy, bright 'twang' effect can be a very useful and effective voice quality when mixed as a component of your voice and has the added benefit of increasing your volume.

This apparent volume increase can really help to lift the level your voice above a band or orchestra due to the band of frequencies which 'twang' boosts. These particular band of frequencies REALLY stand out to the ear and this is why the development of your pharyngeal muscles is a worthy goal which will enable you greater projection of your voice.

Here are some good exercises to build Pharyngeal resonance:

1) Say 'ng' as in the word 'sing' (also used for tone) on a Siren.
2) Say 'Nei' in a whiney style on an octave or circular scale.
3) Sing 'yeah, yeah, yeah' emphasising the 'ee' vowell in a whiney style.

Singing the 'Ng' starting with a tiny small sound and then opening from the 'ng' to any vowell will improvement your placement and resonance and is the original key to isolating and developing your pharyngeal resonance.

Resonators

Resonators are chambers in your body where sound vibrates when you speak or sing. The shape of the resonating space combined with the pitches and vowells you sing is what literally shapes the sound.

There are three main resonators you need to be aware of and they can be simplified to Chest, mouth and head. As everyone's body shape is slightly different and unique to them, so is the sound of each unique voice. Another great reason to be different and unique!

Your chest resonator tends to resonate and amplify lower pitches and wide vowells more so than high pitches and narrow vowells.

Your 'pharynx' (at the back of your mouth, top of the throat) as we just mentioned with pharyngeal muscles could be considered as the most important resonator. This pharygeal cavity extends from the top of the trachea and oesophagus, past the epiglottis and root of your tongue to the region behind your soft pallette. It's important because of it's size, position and degree you can adjust it. As we just demonstrated with the Pharyngeal exercises, this in itself is a powerful and versatile resonator. Other contributors are the position of the tongue, position of the soft palette and altering height of the larynx.

Your head resonator includes the nasal cavity behind the mask of your face and the vibration of bones of your head and these tend to resonate and amplify the higher pitches and narrow vowells by comparison.

Each resonance space makes sympathetic sound vibrations depending on the pitch and vowell being sung. More on using vowells as an effective tool later.

Anchoring Muscles

'Anchoring' is a technique which involves what's known as 'non-violent tension.' Anchoring is the engaging of certain muscle groups to provide you with more support in your singing. It's especially more useful for extra support for powerful singing.

To simplify this, the main areas where anchoring is useful are within the neck, the back, abdominal muscles in front of your stomach and intercostal muscles between your ribs.

a) The Vocal tract - These are Sternocleidomastoid muscles, let's just call them SCM's for short! ...and semispinalis capitas). SCM's stabilise your vocal tract from the sides of the neck whilst the Semispinalis stablises from the back of the neck.

Here are some exercises for you to explore these muscles for anchoring.

1) While standing, stretch to lengthen your spine and pull back slightly, feeling for the large bump of your atlas joint with one hand and the axis joint with the other hand. Aim to bring these these joints into line and then take your hands away, keeping this anchored position for your neck.

2) While keeping your head straight and level above your shoulders, place the palm of your hand flat on the crown of your head. Now push down a little with your hand and as you do, push up a little with your head, keeping your neck in line with your spine. Removing your hand, keep that muscle engagement.

3) Imagine putting on a tight swimming cap. As you're pulling it onto your head, push your head upwards into the cap. Once the imaginary cap is on try to keep this sense of a lengthened neck.

4) Feel the large muscles around the side of your neck (SCM's) with your hand. With the other hand make a fist and press your fist against your forehead. Push back against your fist with your forehead and you'll begin to feel the SCM's working.

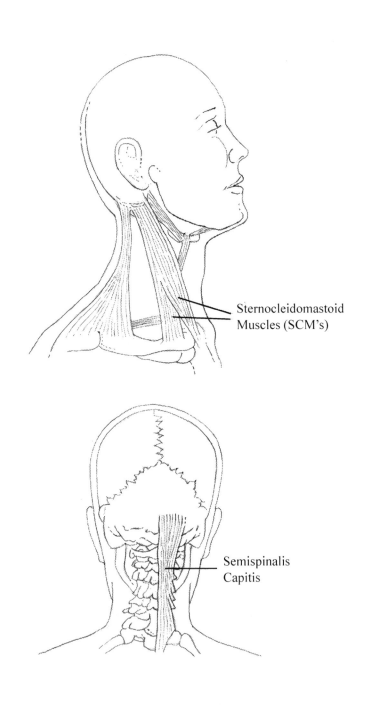

Sternocleidomastoid
Muscles (SCM's)

Semispinalis
Capitis

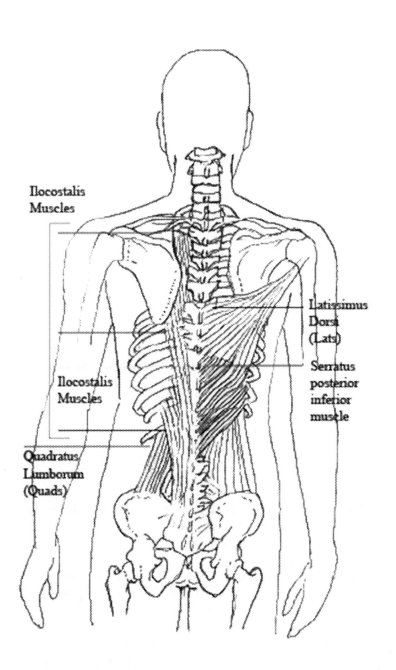

Ilocostalis
Muscles

Ilocostalis
Muscles

Quadratus
Lumborum
(Quads)

Latissimus
Dorsi
(Lats)

Serratus
posterior
inferior
muscle

Anchoring Muscles (continued)

b) The Torso - Muscles of the back. These are Latissimus Dorsi and Quadratus Lumborum) - Lets abbreviate these to 'Lats' and 'Quads.' Other muscles involved are Iliocostalis and Serratus Posterior Inferior.

In anchoring your Torso, these are muscles you can use to stablise your body. They are attached to the spine, the ribs, diaphragm and pelvis so it's no wonder they have an effective stabilising effect.

Alexander work is a method designed to develop human-friendly posture for physical activities. Alexander technique teaches the importance of stabilising 'the back' of our torso so that 'the front' can pull up and the contents of abdomen move back. This creates ultimate anchoring and support for your breath control and contribute to energetic expiration when singing.

Here are some exercises for you to explore these muscles for anchoring.

1) Stand with your feet comfortably apart and soft in the knees (not locked).

Turn your arms outwards in their sockets, keeping them close to you. This fixes the top Lats. Keep your lats fixed as you pull down and out, working from your armpits into your upper back.

2) This exercise is about anchoring for balancing the body and is done with a partner:

(i) Face your partner and make sure you're both standing with your spine upright and in line with your neck and pelvis. Your shoulders need to be dropped and knees not locked.

(ii) Hold onto eachothers forearms, elbows crooked at 90 degrees and hold your partners arms just above the wrists and keep your elbows close in to your sides, arms not locked. Now take it in turns to pull, one against the other.

(iii) Take it in turns to be either the 'puller' or the 'anchorer.' If you're anchoring you need to avoid pulling with your arms and focus the work in the back of your body. So think of bringing your elbows backwards to anchor these back muscles. As the puller, you need to create just enough resistance to engage the muscles but not too much or else you'll both lock up instead.

3) A variation of exercise two. Again stand opposite your partner with your elbows crooked at 90 degrees as before.

Keeping your palms flat, place your hands inside or outside your partners hands. Now one of you pushes out away with the backs of your hands while the other resists with palms.

As with Exercise 2, be aware of making just enough resistance to engage the anchoring muscles (Lats, Quads etc).

Voice Qualities

You've probably heard singers who sing in a variety of textures or styles of voicing and these different voicings can create a good range of dynamics that make exciting vocal performances.

There are five different voice qualities commonly used in popular or commercial music. Practising a range of voice qualities will help you become a far more versatile singer.

So I encourage you to experiment with each of them and try them all. What I'm including here are some auditory cues for you to follow to try them for yourself. There are training sessions and classes that enable you to work on developing each of these and they can be richly rewarding but I hope these cues will give you a good feel and taste of each so you can incorporate them in your singing. The key to using voice qualities is simply choosing where they can best fit with a song or style you're working with but some styles such as Rock or Soul use elements of them all.

Lee Risdale

Speech Quality

Speech Quality is the same quality of voicing we mostly use to speak with. There is no added effect. It's simply your speaking tone except sustained to singing on pitch. The essence of good speech quality though for long-lasting and healthy singing makes good use of a glottal onset of tone. This means that there is good vocal fold closure to achieve a balanced and clear tone which has full body, efficiency of breath and cord adduction. This will enable your voice to be durable because a balanced voice is both healthy and durable.

There are stylistic variation to this though and your singing style or speaking style might not be pure tone. If your voice is breathy or raspy by habit this can be a unique part of your personal speech quality style. Just be aware that if you're not using a balanced, clear tone by choice or default your voice might need a little more vocal care and more of a warm-up and warm-down to preserve it.

Speech Quality is the most common voice quality and the essence of Speech Level Singing which was introduced by Seth Riggs which teaches that singing should be as straight forward as speech, provided that you maintain good cord adduction and neutral larynx position.

Twang Quality

'Twang' is a voice quality that has also been called 'The Singer's formant.' This is because the sound frequencies produced by this voice quality are of a particular distinctive band of harmonics or formants that really stand out to the human ear. For this reason when you sing with Twang the ear of your listener comes out to meet you.

The sound of Twang in it's purest form is bright, brassy and metallic. It can be used to extremes or used sparingly and you can control this. At it's most extreme it can sound very trebly, whiny and exuberant but even when blended in as a component it can boost your volume significantly by up to 20 decibels.

So in adding more twang to your sound you're far more likely to be heard over the band or orchestra and it has the advantage of enabling you to add more volume when needed safely without strain.

Twang is made by a tightening of muscles which contract at the back of your larynx. This wrapping and tightening is made by the aryepyglottic muscle and the Oblique aryetenoid muscle. The Aryepiglottic fold narrows the space directly above your vocal folds creating a narrower funnel and laser-like focused depth of tone. The narrowing of the space and tightening of the 'twanger' creates more twang quality which greatly increases volume with less effort. The closer the Aryetenoid cartilages get to the lower part of the epiglottis the more twanged the sound will become.

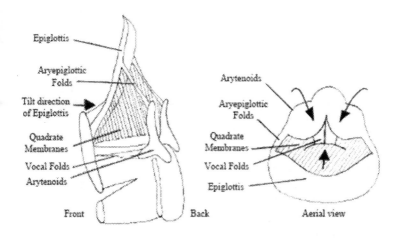

If your voice is quite breathy by habit it's wise to work on developing good balance of breath and good vocal fold closure first (See Tone) before attempting twang to make efficient use of it. Good vocal cord closure comes first.

If you have 'pressed phonation' which means over-compression of your vocal folds it's better to address this first by developing a lighter cord closure using the fine edges of your folds before adding twang or it can overload your voice further. Sirening gently on an 'Oo' vowell may help with this.

If your natural voice quality is 'twangy' already you might find the need to work in the other direction. So to enable you to soften the twang quality try lowering your larynx slightly by sirening down to a low note and maintain this lower position. Holding this lower laryngeal position will help you to let go of the muscles which tighten to make twang.

Let's get a feeling of 'twang' by getting you using these pharyngeal muscles.

Twang Auditory Cues:

1) Say Nyeeeoww like a hungry cat (Notice where you feel the effort).

2) Say Nah-haa-haa-haa-haa like a wicked witch or an evil villain.

3) Immitate the sound of a Police siren sliding up and down on 'ee' or 'ae.'

4) Say 'nyet' on mid to high pitches in your range.

Now try these exercises:

1) Sing Nei, Nei Nei on an Octave Repeater scale.

2) Sing Naa, Naa, Naa on an Octave Repeater scale.

3) Sing 'Ny, Ny, Ny on an Octave Repeater scale.

Bring your full awareness to where you 'feel' the effort. The 'leaning in' of your Epiglottis and the slight tightening of the pharyngeal muscles which you feel at the back of your throat creates 'twang' quality and using pharyngeal muscles is a big contributor to developing greater volume and projection.

The Aryepiglottic fold narrows the space directly above your vocal folds creating a narrower whirlwind funnel of sound that is more metallic, brassy and laser-like is sound quality. Just as a brass instrument projects distinctively this same effect enables your voice to project these bright and exuberant qualities.

Falsetto Quality

You might have heard the term 'Falsetto' banded around quite a lot in vocal auditions or TV Shows. It's commonly thought to be very high in pitch but this isn't entirely true.

Falsetto in itself is a very breathy voice quality. When a singer is in Falsetto their vocal folds are in a 'raised plane' position and vibrating only on the very edges so that the sound quality is very light and has less tone. It's not fully connected to your supporting muscles which engage lower in your body and for this reason there is little body of tone or volume by comparison. Despite this, when singing in this voice quality is done well it can sound fantastic.

Falsetto is therefore a 'breathy' quality in high or low range... although it's more often referred to when a singer is in that light breathy, higher pitched tonality. Breathy speech quality tends to work better in the lower third of a singer's range so you might want to modify your quality to a breathy Speech quality if singing in the lower part of your range.

It can be heard in many genres of music. From Blues to Soul to Pop and Jazz. Sometimes a singer disconnects from their full tone into falsetto as a stylistic effect. Other times it can be used as an introduction or dynamic effect and sometimes singers use it throughout a song. Listen to "Kiss" by Prince. If you listen carefully you can hear how Prince can switch between Falsetto and a lightly connected head voice to increase his dynamic and project those high notes with more energy.

When you sing Falsetto, your folds are vibrating on just the edges to create the breathy disconnected tone where we hear more of the airflow than the tone itself. The ratio of 'airflow to tone' might appear to be something like 80:20. That's 80% air and 20% tone quality.

Falsetto Auditory Cues:

1. Speak/Sing in a forced whisper.

2. Sing a high-pitched, breathy 'Oo.'

3. Imitate the sound of a hooting Owl.

4. Keep this 'hooty' voice quality and say 'Yoo-hoo.'

Cry Quality

Have you ever heard a singer who sings with such expression and emotion that it seems as though they're crying into the notes.

Yes, in a sense they actually are... and this is the essence of Cry voice quality.

When we 'cry' or express our words with great empathy and compassion we access a different voice quality which is embedded into our muscle memory by instinct.

The most expressive singers from Soul singers to Pop to Indie to Rock all use it and it's a big secret to unlocking your voice. When I say secret I mean that there are hidden benefits to crying on pitch.

The first benefit is that singing with Cry adds another deeper dimension of expression and emotion to your singing, a very sincere leaning of tone and timbre which enhances basic speech quality.

The second benefit is that crying on pitch has an anatomical effect that makes it easier to sing through trickier transitions in vocal range (bridges) and makes it easier to sing high notes without strain.

I'd like to cover the two key questions on Cry as a voice quality here. How does it work and how can I do it?

Cry quality is activated by a movement of the thyroid cartilage which is the upper part of the larynx. For this reason the technique is sometimes known as 'Thyroid tilt.' The Thyroid cartilage is the upper part of the larynx which is a bony structure more visibly recognised as the 'Adam's apple.' The Thyroid cartilage houses your vocal cords and a number of larynx muscles which can enhance the sound of the tone-making process. Below the Thyroid cartilage is a second cartilage known as the Cricoid cartilage. It is the Thryroid cartilage action of tilting in relation to the Cricoid which creates a shortening of the vocal cords. This shortening of the cords creates a more flexible platform for your singing. It not only alters the timbre and expression of your tone. It also makes it easier for the singing of higher notes or for bridging the more tricky parts of our vocal range. For these reasons cry is more much more than simply a beautiful tool for expression. It assists a singer in meeting the demands of challenging songs.

How can I make Cry Quality?

Cry auditory Cues:

1. Taunt like a naughty child "Nyea-Nyea-Nyea-Nyea-Nyea."

2. Meow like a hungry cat. "Nyeoow."

3. Moan like a ghost in a haunted house.

4. Speak with empathy as if consoling a crying child.

5. Sustain a note as if immitating a 'crying' Opera singer.

These auditory cues will help you to access thyroid tilt and become more aware of this change of larynx position, especially how it feels so you can anchor it into your muscle memory.

Listen recordings of singers who use a lot of 'crying on pitch.' Which singers do it and do some use it more than others?

Now take one of your favourite songs and practice the Cry technique. You can begin by immitating if you like. Acting is a big part of embedding this voice quality. 'Cry' into every note. Now sing it again in 'Speech quality.' Record yourself if you can singing the same song or part both in 'Speech quality' and then in 'Cry quality' and notice the difference. How does it feel? How does it sound?

It might take some time to really master 'Cry quality' while still keeping good pitch control and this is ok. Be patient and persistent with it and it will undoubtedly get better.

Let's recap. The 'tilted thyroid' gives us the sweet, crying tone. It helps in developing a pleasant vibrato. It can also aid in smoothing out those register shifts (breaks or passagio). Practice engaging the cricothyroid muscle and tilt the thyroid by adopting a posture of crying or sobbing, making a soft whimpering noise, like a puppy whining. The neutral thyroid gives us a more speechy quality but when 'tilted' the thyroid cartilage influences not only pitch but also the quality and intensity of the sound you produce.

You'll find a lot of Cry in Blues, Soul and Jazz styles but it's prevalent in all styles. Here are just some singers who have used 'crying on pitch' a lot in their singing. Marvin Gaye, Tom Jones, Christna Aguilera, Adele, Amy Winehouse, Seal, Joss Stone, Cee Lo Green, Robert Plant, Paul Rodgers.

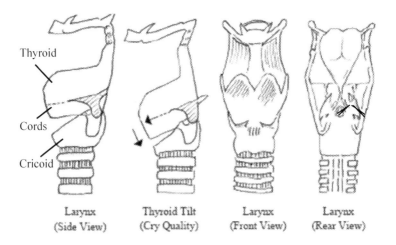

Thyroid

Cords

Cricoid

| Larynx | Thyroid Tilt | Larynx | Larynx |
| (Side View) | (Cry Quality) | (Front View) | (Rear View) |

Cry technique or 'Thyroid Tilt' could be one of the most valuable skills for you to master as a singer because it has so many advantages and benefits. These include enrichment of tone, more ease and flexibility as well as increased ability to sing higher and through bridges without excess tension. Cry quality singers also sound the most expressive.

The sound of Cry quality itself can transform a performance. To illustrate this, here are sketches of the larynx from various angles.

1. Larynx (Side view) - This shows the larynx in neutral or rested position. Your larynx assumes this position for speaking or singing in Speech quality. The dotted line represents the vocal cords position within the larynx.

2. Thyroid tilt (Cry quality) - This shows the affect of crying on pitch. The Thyroid cartilage tilts forward hinged from the Cricoid in a tilting and rocking motion. This action stretches and shortens the thickness of the cords/folds enabling more flexibility in making higher pitches and is help negotiating bridges of the voice. The Cricoid also has the flexibility to tilt away (which is helpful for safe belting) and can be felt when you make a big yawn.

3. Larynx (Front View) - Use your fingers gently against your neck to feel these two bumps and 'V' shape in the front of your thyroid/ or "adams apple."

4. Larynx (Rear View) - Shows the Epiglottis that drops to help you swallow your food (and assists with Twang) plus vocal folds opening from the back.

Chapter Nine

Vibrato

What is vibrato?

Vibrato is the slight fluctuation of pitch or tremor we can hear when a voice is sustaining a note. It is a very natural phenomenon and although most voices tend to have it quite naturally there are some bad habits that can make it sound not so good. So what we'll cover here are examples of the pitfalls and how to check if your vibrato is working at it's best.

So, here's the science part...True vibrato is naturally produced within your larynx. It's produced by the enervation of the superior laryngeal nerve to the Cricothyroid muscle.

This tensing and relaxing pattern is called a physiological tremor rate. What does this mean?

One way to explain it is that it's the same response that happens when you've lifted something heavy and your muscles start to tremble. Your larynx is stabilising to deal with the airflow pressure against your vocal cords as they resist the increased airflow and this is what creates the vibrato effect. It's a normal balancing between tensing and relaxing within your voice.

The vibrato fluctuates the pitch by a semi-tone and back again many times per second and each fluctuation is called an undulation or cycle.

The best sounding vibrato rate is where it fluctuates by 6-6.5 cycles per second. Sometimes up to 8 cycles per second. In Operatic singing, a heavier vocal production tends to produce a slower rate of 5-6 cycles per second.

There are two main dysfunctional vibratos that should be avoided or can be modified if you use them.

Straight tone (No Vibrato) -A straight tone shows little or no evidence of vibrato and inhibits the tremor rate. It can sometimes cause tension and tiredness in your voice. If this is you, try relaxing more when you sing. Take time to take a good low breath and make sure your stomach/abs are relaxed on the in-breath. Don't pull your stomach in. Also experiment with singing trills, quick shifts in pitch to experience your voice shake.

Here is another way to experience vibrato if you have a straight tone. Sing a sustained note and as you do so use your forefinger to push in just above your abdominals, just below your breastbone. Try to push in at around 6 times per second and you can clearly hear the tremor vibrato effect and allow it to begin to sink into your muscle memory. Next try adjusting your breath control so that your breath is inhaled low into your body and fully supported by your diaphragm. Your abs and the intercostal muscles between your ribs should generate enough balanced airflow to produce your vibrato more naturally.

Trillo is a faster vibrato which can sound like a bleating sound. It's in the range of 8-12 cycles per second and it's sometimes also known as jutter or bleat. The cause of Trillo is either abdominal tension or laryngeal tension at the vocal folds. It sounds as a very fast vibrato which has can also have an irregular rate. This can be corrected with patience and persistence. If this is you, work at relaxing your breath support, relaxing your abdominal muscles as you inhale and practice creating a smooth phonation of tone when sustaining a note. You can use an Edgy 'Mm' or 'Nng' to develop this smooth tone.

Tremelo or wobble is heard when your vibrato is too slow. This happens because of three possible reasons. A lack of physical exercise, a lack of singing exercise or too much airflow/heavy voice production. If this is you, get some regular exercise to increase your core body strength, especially your abdominal muscles.

Use a regular vocal exercise routine to keep your voice in shape or work with a vocal coach and try to practice and perform regularly. Ensure you don't take in too much air and don't stack it up. Habitual heavy use of airflow adds too much weight and pressure to your voice. Remember that a small, adequate low breath goes a long way if you control the airflow and support it well. Study and practice Speech Level Singing or Bel Canto to bring balance to your voice. A balanced breath control where your vocal cords can comfortably resist the level of airflow makes for a healthy sounding tone and will sustain you for life in your singing.

Vibrato Task: Record yourself singing a sustained note. Listen back and consider your own vibrato rate. Does in sound fast, slow, regular or is it missing? Hum a pitch. Does it start straight and stay straight? Does it start straight and vibrate towards the end? Does the cycle rate change or does it sound regular? Make yourself aware of your own vibrato.

Chapter Ten

Articulation & Enunciation

There are various alternative definitions of the term 'articulation' and here are a just few of them:

1. Clarity in the production of successive musical notes.
2. The way in which you pronounce words or produce sounds.
3. The act of expressing something in a coherent verbal form.
4. An aspect of pronunciation involving the articulatory organs.

Articulation comes from the Latin word for "jointed" or "divided into joints." It's commonly used in singing to emphasise the use of vowells and consonants.

Enunciation is the act of pronouncing words. Enunciation comes from the Latin word enuntiationem, meaning "declaration."

We do this using vowells and consonants. So in this chapter I'm going to share some great tools and exercises to make the best of singing your vowells and consonants effectively which can make a significant enhancement to your singing.

Vowells

Vowell sounds are the sustained free-flowing singing tones we make.

We make them by forming our mouth space and using our articulators which are; the tongue, lips, jaw teeth, hard palate and soft palate.

The first thing to emphasise is that you need to have the tip of your tongue lightly touching your bottom front row of teeth when singing a vowell unless you're articulating a consonant such as 'G' or 'Guh.' When our tongue pull backwards in the mouth it causes an obstruction to producing the vowell successfully and blocks resonance or with focus of sound.

Read out the phonetic alphabet below and say it clearly out loud. Notice how, in saying these in a progressive order - The back of your tongue begins in a high position (ee) and gradually lowers in position to lie flatter from the back to the tip.

International Phonetic Alphabet

'ee' as in see [i]

'ih' as in it [I]

'eh' as in end [ɛ]

'aa' as in at [æ]

'a' as in day [ɛɪ]

'ah' as in far [c]

'uh' as in up [ʌ]

'aw' as in dawn [ɔ]

'uu' as in book [U]

'oo' as in soon [ʊ]

When your mouth is widened toward a smile it helps you to create a 'mask resonance' which produces great overtones from your head and nasal cavity. Be sure that if you use this you don't pull your lips back or over-use a smile as it can activate further muscles that can disturb your tone. When singing on a low pitch you can brighten your vowell sound by widening your mouth space horizontally as in smiling to create an upper resonance and keep a good 'mask placement.'

With the vowells 'ee' ih' and 'oo' we tend to close our jaw and throat space. This can be problematic when singing 'ee' at a highish pitch. A good general rule is that high and loud tones need more resonating space so relax your tongue slightly as in singing 'ih'and open your jaw a little more to enable you to sing a clear and open vowell.

Vowell Exercises

1. Open your mouth about an inch and a half (about two finger widths) and touch your fingertips against your chin to help your jaw stay open. Then say: ah... ah (as in far) into... eeeeee (as in see).

Notice your tendancy to close your jaw on the "ee" vowel sound.

2. Repeat, keeping the same open space you feel on the "ah" vowel right through the "ee" vowel. Say the "ee" with the tip of the tongue touching the backs of the lower front teeth.

3. Repeat the exercise for both the "ih" and the "oo" vowels sounds.

ah ...ah ... iiiiiih (as in it)

ah ...ah ... ooooooo (as in soon)

If you're a singer who sings primarily in head voice or upper register, these following exercises will be helpful in developing a clear and well-projected tone. The upper register or head voice also plays a valuable role in the development of the lower register or chest voice.

The upper register may be used as an upward extension of the chest voice quality, or "high mix." Use these exercises to strengthen your upper register. "ee" is a good practice vowel for this purpose.

4. On a siren-like "ee" sound, try this:

ee ... ee ... eeeeeeeeeeeeeeeeeeeeee (slide up - slide down).

5. Now follow the "ee" vowel with other vowel sounds beginning with "eh" (as in end), like this:

ee ... ee ... eeeh (as in hen)
ee ... ee ... eeah (as in hot)
ee ... ee ... eeuh (as in love)
ee ... ee ... eeaw (as in dawn)
ee ... ee ... eeuuh (as in book)
ee ... ee ... eeoo (as in you)

6. Now, using what you've learned about breath support, focusing and open space, make the scale part of the second part of the phrase to a five tone scale (half of the major scale up & down) as smooth as the slide that you sing before it.

7. Repeat the same exercise, using "aa" on the slide and the following vowel sounds on the scale.

(slide) a-a-a-a ... (scale) a-a-a-a-ah (as in hot)
(slide) a-a-a-a... (scale) u-u-u-u-uh (as in love)
(slide) a-a-a-a... (scale) a-a-a-a-aw (as in dawn)
(slide) a-a-a-a... (scale) u-u-u-u-uh (as in book)
(slide) a-a-a-a... (scale) o-o-o-o-oo (as in you)

(slide) a-a-a-a... (scale) e-e-e-e-eh (as in hen)
(slide) a-a-a-a... (scale) e-e-e-e-ee (as in he)

Be sure that you keep the focus and the forward placement that you feel on the "aa" sound in the vowel sound that follows it.

Diphthongs (double vowel sounds)

A diphthong is a combination vowel, actually two vowel sounds back to back.

For singing, "y" is pronounced as "ee" (as in see). "You" is pronounced, ee-oo. The "w" is pronounced as "oo" (as in soon). "Want" is pronounced, oo- ah-nt. The voiceless "wh" sound (as in where) works better for singing as the voiced "w" ("oo").

In some vocal styles, the last part of the diphthong can be held longer. In Country music, for example, the word "day" may sometimes be sung as - "deheeee." Most often though, softening the "ee" at the end of the

word by pronouncing "ih" (as in it) instead of "ee" (as in see). d-eh-ih sounds much better. You may choose to soften the "oo" in "Go" (G-uh-oo) by pronouncing it "uu" (as in book) instead of "oo" (as in soon). It really does depend on the style of music you're singing as well as your own personal style.

Consonants

Consonant sounds are formed by the movement or position of our articulators. They help make words clear. If you don't articulate them properly they interfere with the focus of the tone and forward placement, blocking the free flow of sound.

So here is another excellent secret to great singing. In placing more emphasis on the articulation of some consonants you can...

1. Create better clarity of your song lyrics.

2. Create more 'compression' which makes singing easier.

The first part in achieving greater clarity may seem straight forward. It can be frustrating when listening to a singer if we can barely make out a word they're singing. When we're hearing a variety of vowels but no consonants they could be singing in any language that we fail to recognise. Getting your articulators to really work makes a great difference to a performance. Listen to any great singer. A good example is anything recorded by Sam Cooke. He pulls in his listener with crisp and well-delivered consonants that tell a clear soulful story, whether in either a smooth or raucous delivery.

Good articulation of consonants, particularly c, d. g, k, l. m, n, p, w consonants creates a confined internal pressure or 'compression' which enables your vocal cords to phonate well to produce a well defined tone.

This means that when you really articulate a consonant with good breath support and energy it's the equivalent of an athlete using a springboard to clear the long jump at the olympics. It greatly assists your delivery and control of your singing. It's like giving a tightrope walker a nice balanced pole to help steady their balance. Many of the best vocal exercises use consonants as grips or stabilisers to train and balance our vocal tone before 'taking the stabilisers off our bike' and singing phrases with vowels alone (without the assistance of consonants). So when you're singing make good use of the consonants. Here are some exercises to give your articulators a good workout.

Consonant Exercises:

Try each of these tongue twisters with special emphasis to the consonants. Start slowly at first and really use your articulators to pronounce each clearly.

Betty bought butter, but the butter was bitter. So Betty bought better butter to make the bitter butter better.

Lee Risdale

Peter Piper picked a peck of pickled peppers. If Peter Piper picked a peck of pickled peppers, where's the peck of pickled peppers Peter Piper picked?

Red lorry yellow lorry, red lorry yellow lorry.

Round the rugged rocks the ragged rascal ran.

She sells sea shells by the sea shore.

Six Sicillian sea-men sailed the seven seas.

Something stirred the hissing snake from it's silent slumber.

Tie a knot, tie a knot. Tie a tight, tight knot. Tie a knot in the shape of a nought.

Mama say mama sah ma-ma cu-sa

Voiced and Voiceless Consonants

Place your fingertips at the front of your throat and say "zzzz" (as in the word 'zoo'), with a strong buzzing sound. That vibration you feel against your fingertips is from your vibrating vocal cords. The voiced consonant requires your vocal cords to focus and vibrate producing the voiced sound.

Now, place your fingertips at the front of your throat and say "ssss" (as in song), with a good, strong hissing sound. Notice there is no vibration against your fingertips. Voiceless consonants require the vocal cords to open and not vibrate. ("voiceless").

Voiceless consonants create a gap in the stream of vocal tone by requiring the vocal cords to part. With your fingertips at your throat, say "the zoo" and then say "with Sue". Notice the interruption of vibration during the "ssss" in "Sue". The vocal cords un-focus for voiceless consonants.

Because your vocal cords are open for the voiceless consonants, they have a tendency to stay partially open during the vowel that follows. This creates breathiness and loss of projection and might causes the voice to "crack". A good way to train yourself to reduce this tendency is to think the voiced consonant counterpart and to immediately focus the vocal cords for the vowel. 'Think' the focused vowel before you pronounce the consonant. When moving from a vowel to a consonant, don't anticipate the consonant by shortening the duration of the vowel and don't alter the vowel sound as you approach the consonant. Moving your articulators too early toward the consonant position interferes with focus and closes the resonating space too soon.

Silent H

"H" is a voiceless consonant that doesn't require a specific action of the articulators. The 'Silent H' is a useful device as a softer opening into your tone and if you're avoiding a glottal attack.

If you're voicing 'Combined Consonants' make sure to pronounce the combination correctly. Some examples are where an "s" following a voiced consonant is pronounced "zz" as in 'dogs' and an "s" following a voiceless consonant is pronounced "ss" as in 'pets.'

You can feel your vocal cords alternately focus and de-focus in the next exercise. Both consonants in each pair require the same position of the articulators. But the voiceless consonants "sss" and "fff" require the vocal cords to be de-focused. Keep a steady flow of air as you alternate between "zzzzzzz" (voiced) and "sssssss" (voiceless).

zzzzzssssszzzzzssssszzzzzsssss

vvvvvfffffvvvvvfffffvvvvvfffff

In the next exercise, match the focus of "aa" (as in at) in the vowel of the word that follows it.

Don't let the consonant bring too much excessive breath into the vocal tone.

aaa … aaa …haaat
aaa … aaa … saaad
aaa … aaa … caaatch
aaa … aaa … scaaat
aaa … aaa … chaaat
aaa … aaa …faaast
aaa … aaa … shaaack

In this next exercise, focus the vowel immediately. Don't allow the voiceless consonant to bring excessive breath into the vocal tone. Use "aa" (as in at).

Choose any one pitch and sing the following:

aa …
ee …
see …
aa …
ih …

fit
aa ...
eh ...

Alternating between voiced and voiceless consonants will bring flexibility to your singing, enabling you to be a more versatile vocalist.

Chapter Eleven

Vowell Modification

Ok, are you ready for this one? Here is one of the key secrets to great singing...We've looked at articulating vowells and practised moving from one vowell shape to another but now for something revolutionary.

Sometimes you can exchange a vowell for a substitute vowell to enable you to sing notes easier and help it sound acoustically better.

This is especially useful when singing through vocal bridges where it can be more difficult to sing freely and easily. The basis of vowell modification is this.

Wide vowells can be exchanged for a narrower vowell as we sing higher pitches, whilst narrow vowells can be exchanged for wider vowells when singing in the lower register.

Wide vowells tend to resonate in the chest so have more chest or bass resonance. Narrow vowells resonate more in the head register and less in the chest so have more head or treble resonance.

The vowell sound or timbre is actually made by the wind pipe which changes shape according the vowell you intend.

To test this, try this simple experiment. Inhale and hold your breath for a few seconds...As you do this, silently mouth the vowells 'A, E, I, O, U.' Flick your neck just to one side of your larynx/adam's apple as you mouth the vowells, whilst holding your breath. Can you hear the timbre change..?

Changing the vowell shape affects the sound and can soften an otherwise harsh tone, channel the sound in a more efficient way that is much friendlier to the singer, helpful in singing through bridges and more friendly to the ears of the listener. Opposite is a Vowell narrowing chart which illustrates problem vowells and the vowell that can be substituted in it's place.

So first, let's establish which are wide or narrow vowells and try this.

Vowell Narrowing Chart

Problem Vowell		Substitute Vowell	
BAT	b [æ] t	BET	b [ɛ] t
BAY	b [ɛɪ] t	BEET	b [i] t
BET	b [ɛ] t	BIT	b [I] t
BEET	b [i] t	BIT	b [I] t
BOAT	b [œ] t	BOOT	b [u] t
BOUGHT	b [ɔ] t	BUT	b [ʌ] t
BUCK	b [ʌ] t	BOOK	b [ʊ] t
BOOK	b [ʊ] t	BOOT	b [u] t

Here are some examples of narrowing problem vowells in classic pop songs.

When a man loves a woman (Percy Sledge) can be sung as:
W[I]n a m[ε]en l[ʌ]ves a w[ʌ]-m[ε]n or ..."Win a men luhves a wuh-men."

Let's stay Together (Al Green) can be sung as:
L[I]t's st[I]y Together or ..."Lit's stiy Together."

Rolling in the Deep (Adele) can be sung as:
We coulda had it [ʌ]ll, rollin' in the D[I]-eep
or ..."We coulda had it uh-ll, rollin' in the Dih-eep."

TASK - Pick your favourite song, especially one where there is a tricky section to sing and try this exercise of narrowing vowels. Which vowels can you substitute? Does it make it easier to sing? In most cases this works brilliantly and is one of the key aspects of great singing.

Narrow the Vowells in the Bridges

The most useful places to replace a vowell with a narrower vowell is in the approach to a vocal bridge. Bridges can vary slightly from singer to singer but as a general guide the first two male bridges begin at around Eb4 and Ab4 (above middle C) whilst female bridges begin around Ab4 and Eb5. Further bridges may typically repeat at around the same intervals distance (Eb and Ab).

Male Singer - First Bridge (Eb4) Second Bridge (Ab4)

Female Singer - First Bridge (Ab4) Second Bridge (Eb5)

The reason that male bridges and female bridges usually begin at the interval of about a fourth (to a fifth) apart in comparison is because the male larynx is larger in size than the female so his ability to access and pitch the same notes requires more gear changes and naturally his bridges start significantly lower. Note: Eb is also written as D#

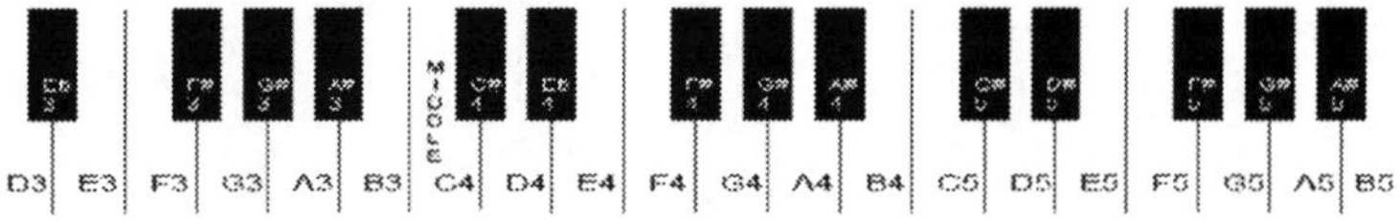
D3
E3
F3
G3
A3
B3
C4
D4
E4
F4
G4
A4
B4
C5
D5
E5
F5
G5
A5
B5

Chapter Twelve

Negotiating Bridges

As a singer ascends up a scale in pitch we can encounter areas where our voice breaks. It can disconnect or sometimes we feel that we have to use more muscular effort in attempt to sing higher. These breaks in the voice are common to every singer and usually occur in predictable places as mentioned before. Traditional classical vocal technique refers to these bridges as passagio. These bridges are 'passages' or areas of 'transition' from one part of your vocal register to another. We feel these transitions as adjustments with our vocal cords and as a shift in resonance. As singers, we often struggle with the problem of how to sing through or cover up these breaks in the voice. There are three most useful tools for singing through Bridges of the voice well so that it's possible with correct training to blend our tone effectively enough through these transitions that the bridges can appear almost seamless.

We could compare it to making a gear change to a 'higher gear' in a motor car because to allow us to make our vocal gear change into another register smoothly we have to do three things at once. It's a bit like taking your foot off the gas, pressing the clutch and moving the gear stick: except we do this...

1) Reduce the amount of airflow / blow less air.
2) Narrow the vowell.
3) Cry on pitch (also known as thyroid tilt - See Cry Quality).

Let's break this down: As you approach a vocal bridge to enable a smooth transition to the next vocal register:

1. Firstly reduce the amount of airflow, which as a result you can use thin cords (rather than a thick vocal cord co-ordination).

2. As you do this, narrow the vowell(s) you're singing. So for example, use the Vowell Chart to change the word 'A-ll' to 'Uh-ll.'

3. Use 'Cry Quality' as your vocal set-up. Crying on pitch will enable your cords to shorten with a thyroid tilt, making them far more flexible to pitch the higher register. Thinking 'whiny' is a good cue for cry quality.

Combining these three techniques will help you to make your transitions far easier and you can begin to develop a good 'Mix' voice which blends chest and head resonances throughout your bridges.

Here is an exercise to practice this over an Octave. Sing an Octave scale as below, male G major / female C major.

Aa - Aa - Ah - Uh (Up the Octave G3 to G4 for male, C4 to C5 female)

Using less airflow as you ascend, while narrowing the vowell here from 'Aa' to 'Uh' as you cry into the pitch will make the transition easier and smoother. Legendary Opera singer, Pavarotti described this as a figure '8.'

Reduce Airflow  Narrow Vowell

Internationally acclaimed Speech Level Singing technique has produced many great award winning singers and is accredited to sustaining their singing careers as well as in live performance. Seth Riggs' legendary work built upon the techniques of Bel Canto and developed SLS technique to cope with the heavy demands placed upon contemporary singers. The technique works brilliantly across all popular genres to develop and maintain healthy vocal pedagogy. I highly recommend you looking into Speech Level Singing training which encourages balanced singing using techniques to sing comfortably through the bridges of the voice without undue tension, using a neutral larynx and balanced tone production. SLS technique develops strength and flexibility in voices after establishing balance of tone throughout an extended vocal range.

Singing Riffs, Trills & Runs

Riffs, trills and runs are the stylistic decorations and vocal embellishments that can inspire a truly remarkable vocal performance. On the positive side, they're the professional touch that can make an amateur singer sound like a note-weilding Jedi master of their voice.

On the flip side they can be over-done and some artistes who over-do it can come across as some kind of note-tastic voice machine. A little annoying. So, good advice here is... Yes, use them but use them wisely. Ideally not in every other phrase. It's good to think of these embellishments as jewellery. A little bling and sparkle can be impressive but too much can come across as in-sincere and can detract from the meaning of a song or vocal performance.

When used sparingly vocal riffs, trills and runs can truly wow your audience and get them to their feet. Firstly let's define what each of these are:

Riffs - A riff is one 'simple melody repeated as a loop' over a number of times in succession as one phrase. Short but repetitive and effective.

Trills - A trill is 'three notes' as often part of a blues scale sung as one quick phrase. The two common types used are ascending trills and descending trills. Trills are most commonly used at the end of a phrase.

Runs - Vocal runs are made from a scale using many notes that are sung as 'one long phrase' in one breath.

There are many great examples of riffs, trills and runs in Classical, Pop, Rock, Soul and Jazz amongst other genres but perhaps there is no other genre that uses them as complex as modern R&B.

You see some singers try to 'run before they can walk' (please excuse the pun). The secret to great riffs, trills and runs is precision and you have to slow them down to start with. Break down the notes and sing them slowly, being careful to pitch each note correctly. Next repeat it to develop the phrasing and then very gradually begin to speed it up. When this is done well we call it good 'delineation.' Delineation is the art of 'stepping' from pitch to pitch precisely yet joining the notes up smoothly and so you need to make conscious practice of 'stepping' the notes and not slurring them.

Here is a task to enable you to develop your delineation.

TASK: Find good examples of Riffs, Trills and Runs in your favourite songs.

Now, listen carefully to the notes that are being sung. Repeat the phrase enough times until you can memorise the notes.

Next sing the notes at half speed/tempo taking care to sing each of the pitches. Be aware of any tendency to slur from pitch to pitch and work at 'stepping' the pitches in a smooth 'legato' phrase.

Now, gradually begin to speed this up, repeating it faster towards the actual tempo. Take care to 'step' the notes and pitch them precisely as you delineate them as one phrase.

Correcting Common Vocal Faults and Tend-to's

When working on correctly vocal faults it's often always best to seek the help of a Vocal Tutor who will be trained in developing your vocal technique.

However, here are some useful pointers that will help guide you in how to overcome common vocal faults which when tackled can greatly improve your singing. Awareness is the first step. We can refer to these vocal faults as 'tend-to's' because they are habits we tend to adopt depending on our speaking voice and tendency, all of which are unique and personal. Although what we refer to here are 'faults' if they inhibit your intention for your own vocal style, in some cases the 'fault' may be the one thing that makes a singer's voice sound unique... It's for this reason that a coach can help in advising what's most beneficial as far as developing technique. As a general rule though, working on these common faults is fundamental to good, healthy singing and sustaining good vocal pedagogy.

Once you're aware of a problem there is always an exercise or solution that can be used to counteract it.

High Breath

If we inhale our breath too high in the body rather than low, it isn't fully connected to the muscles of support (abs and intercostals). This instead encourages you to grip unnecessary larynx and throat/neck muscles in attempt to support your voice. The result of this can be an un-supported, shaky tone that sounds strained. If you can clearly hear the breath coming in as in a 'surprise' breath it's probably too high.

If you feel you do this, counteract the tendency by training in a new habit. Practice taking a 'LOW' breath into your stomach or waist-line. Lie on the floor and place a book on your stomach. Take low breaths and time the exhalation to three times the length of the inhalation. This low breath is supported by your abdominals which 'lean out' on the out-breath and intercostal muscles between your ribs which keep your lower rib-cage out, high and wide.

Pitching problems - Intonation

Ok, so this is possibly the most obvious problem to the listener. Pitching intonation is the result of poor breath support primarily so if you tackle the high breath problem given above by focusing on creating a 'Low breath' habit this will go a long way to improve your pitching.

Having a regular warm-up and exercise regime is also vital to improve and fine-tune your pitching along with your breath control. Make yourself a CD or audio file of vocal exercises you can use each day or before rehearsal or performances and keep it close to you. Regular voice exercise and training will greatly improve your pitch control.

The third aspect of pitch control is awareness. It wasn't until I really began to pay closer attention to my pitching of each note that I really made great headway in pitching more precisely.

When you pay closer attention to it, either by recording and re-recording yourself and being persistent until you get each note right... you're beginning a great habit of awareness which also works it's way into your muscle memory until it will be almost unthinkable for you to sing off-key or pitchy.

Awareness is a big part of developing great pitch control so if you focus on breath control and only this attention to it for a while, you'll notice a great improvement. Also listen closely to the music and develop your audio perception. It may also help you to learn an instrument if you don't already which will help develop your overall musicality and sense of pitch.

Constriction

Constriction is the strained sounding and 'closed-up,' tight vocal sound we sometimes hear from inexperienced rock singers or in extreme vocal styles. It's created by a narrowing of the pharynx and closing 'false' vocal cords which sit above your vocal cords. These 'false cords' are the same muscles we engage when in 'fight or flight mode' or in a fearful situation and they're primarily used for protection. Our ancestors would have engaged these false cords or constricted when 'fighting off a lion' while we most likely engage them when lifting something heavy or protecting our windpipe from receiving food while we're swallowing it.

If you're a Screamo singer or Guttural screamer vocalising extreme rock vocals, constriction might be necessary to achieve that sound. If this is you, try to use it sparingly, especially if you're singing as well. To counteract constriction let's first remember what constriction feels like. Push hard against a wall with all your might. Notice the pressure building in your throat and that tightening. We're going to counter the constriction tendency first by making a big wide yawn. Notice the throat space open up.

Now imagine yourself in a library with a friend. Your friend has just told you something hilarious and you laugh a 'silent laugh' as not to draw attention to yourself and disturb the librarian. Again, notice this feeling at the back of your throat. The technique of 'Belt' voice quality, a loud voice quality has sometimes been described as 'happy yelling' and some singers find this a good term to describe singing out without constriction.

Keep working at retracting your 'false' vocal folds to produce an open, clear tone without any constriction.

Flipping

Flipping is the tendency to flip from a connected tone into a breathy disconnected tone and happens when we sing from a comfortable register into a higher register. This is a common problem related to singing through Bridges in the voice. If you find you're doing this, it will help you to get a good vocal exercise routine such as Speech Level Singing which will train your ability to create balance through your bridges. Successful bridging will counteract this tendency which occurs when our vocal cords don't adduct well on a given note. It's usually because of a bridge or a place in range where you are not used to singing or speaking so it's not trained into your muscle memory (yet). But here's the thing - You can improve it and develop it with exercises.

If you work at 'mixing' chest and head resonance through edgy and pharyngeal vocal exercises such as whiny 'Nei, Nuh and No' using various scales this will also counteract a tendency to flip and help keep you connected.

Develop a good vocal exercise regime or work with a coach to help extend your range and counteract your tendancy to flip.

Pressed Phonation

Pressed Phonation happens when vocal cords are slamming into each other and working very hard to deal with a very high airflow or increased airflow. Sometimes this happens when we blow too much air and our cords are working really hard to deal with the airflow - They over-work or over-compensate and can create a very distorted tone.

To counteract this tendency work on creating more balance in your voice. Develop your ability to bridge through registers and to sing which a balanced airflow, supported and connected. Work at producing a clear, easy tone at low volume by simply humming a 'Mmm' or 'Nng' or 'Oo' in an exercise, as a siren or with a song. Creating a light but distinct smooth tone throughout your range will make you a more versatile singer and counteract a tendency to 'over-press' with your vocal cords. Work at developing your clear, easy, pure tone.

Although gradual 'leaning in' with cords is useful later to increase strength and flexibility and is the basis of a great Mix voice, this can be done effectively only when balance is achieved throughout your range first so get the balance right first.

Chapter Thirteen

Practice Routine

Why have a practice routine?

We've established in this Body section of the book that we Singer's need regular vocal exercise to both maintain and develop our physical muscles. You can create your own practice routine or devise one with a Vocal tutor or coach. The important thing is using something regularly that will warm-up your voice gradually and keep it in good shape. For this I'm going to give examples of voice exercises used in Speech Level Singing which effectively covers all vocal styles.

A good practice routine should ideally have three parts:

1) The Warm-up.

2) Exercises that develop strength and flexibility.

3) Application - Songs.

The warm-up should include exercises that are designed to warm-up your voice gradually and without undue tension. For example:

Lip Roll scales and sirens
Edgy 'Mmm' Humming and 'Ng' for tone building

Next use The Vocal exercises to develop balance, strength and flexibility. For example:

Guh, Gi, Go (Octave or Circular 1.5 octave scale)
Nei (Octave or Circular 1.5 octave scale)
Muh (Octave or Circular 1.5 octave scale and sustained notes)
Sirens (Slide up from a note to it's octave, or up two octaves and back down)

Balancing 'G' exercises are great for balancing our voice - Adding a 'G' consonant before the 'uh' vowel helps to balance the airflow and tone of notes throughout your range.

This is otherwise known as registration as the goal is to balance notes equally in tone and volume throughout vocal registers. 'Muh' vocal exercise tool works at the goal of a low (neutral) and stable larynx.

Mix tool exercises such as 'Nei' help to mix your chest and head registers and blend between registers. Sirens are another great way to blend registers and develop control and balance.

Song Application - Now that you've warmed up and exercised your voice, it's time to apply yourself to the expressive and challenging art of singing songs. If you're new to singing choose songs that you love but feel comfortable for you to sing. Also, if you're able to, transpose your favourite song to a more manageable key.

If you're working on cover songs from your band's set list, listen passively and then objectively to the structure and then the vocal phrasing and expression of the vocal before you begin singing. This will make sure you pick up all of the stylistic nuances which you can then adapt more successfully. Listen to the song on repeat if possible to soak it up.

If you're working on your own original songs, slow them down for the sake of your practice to enable you to get a better handle on your pitching and vocal phrasing as well as how you can creatively develop it vocally both stylistically and expressively.

This three part vocal routine described, combining an effective warm-up followed by vocal exercises and song-work is a professional win-win for vocalists.

The Benefit of Vocal Exercises

Each of the common vocal faults which we highlighted in the previous section can be counteracted effectively with a great system of vocal exercises:

Visit my website to access many of the great vocal exercises there. Better still get yourself regular voice lessons with a coach who encourages you and has your best interests at heart to enable you to achieve your goals.

Use Vocal Exercises to:

1. Develop greater breath control.

2. Create balance throughout your range so that each note can be sung at the same level volume - registration.

3. Build strength and flexibility.

4. Develop your ability to negotiate bridges and create good 'Mix' voice.

5. Extend your vocal range.

Chapter Seventeen

Vocal Health

Ok, so I was going to list do's and don'ts but let's be quirky and list them as 'Voice-lovers' and 'Voice-killers.' In truth the Voice-killers won't kill your voice in the short-term (although I've heard one guys voice disappear into two songs after a shot of whiskey) but they will affect your performance and possibly damage your voice in the long-term.

Best advice is to avoid eating for up to an hour before rehearsing or performing and drink only water when you're singing to keep you hydrated. Your voice can be very resilient and self-healing but it's also a delicate instrument that can be permanently damaged if you don't take care of it. It's important to trust the signs of a weary voice and give it rest when needed as well as regular exercise to keep it healthy. Here follows a list of 'voice-lovers' and 'voice killers.'

There are naturally a list of do's and don'ts for best vocal health and this becomes more apparent when you're singing and performing regularly. It's really about taking care of your voice long-term but also keeping it in good shape so you can sing at your best and have stamina to sing for longer. So here follows a list of 'Voice-lovers' and 'voice-killers.'

Voice-lovers

Water - H20 is without doubt what singers need the most. Our bodies are comprised mainly of water and we need to keep our vocal cords hydrated during all of that singing. No other drink will do it as well.

Wholegrains, Fruits and Vegetables - These foods contain high levels of Vitamins A, C and E – Vitamin A helps cells regenerate normally, Vitamin C helps prevent the common cold and sore throat as well as improve immune functions of the body, and Vitamin E is a powerful anti-oxidant that protects cell membranes and also improves immune functions of the body.

Honey - Manuka Honey has anti-microbial properties. This means that bacteria will find it hard to survive and reproduce in honey. This also means that when we have a sore throat or just feel some discomfort in our voice, we can just take one spoonful of pure Manuka Honey, and let it drizzle down our throat. This will help to keep the bacteria away, and will also help our sore throat to heal faster. Manuka Honey has yet another great healing property, which is that it is antiseptic and anti-inflammatory! This means that it will help to prevent any infection from spreading, and will thus speed up the recovery of our sore throat.

Sleep - Try to get eight hours of sleep each night if you can. Our bodies need sleep more than we realise and it can really affect our voice if we haven't had enough rest. It's like running on an empty gas tank. Try to get a good nights sleep before a performance and if you have problems sleeping,

Warm-up - Use exercises to warm-up your voice gradually. Start with Lip rolls or gentle humming to viesel-dilate those vocal cords.

Ginger - Another de-flammatory food. Go buy your ginger root now! If not a packet of Ginger nut biscuits will have to do. 'Honey, lemon and Ginger tea' is also very good and has a great taste.

Throat-Coat Herbal Tea- Ingredients include Licorice root, marshmallow root and Slippery Elm bark which has been proven to contain voice nourishing properties. A sweet tea, from Oregon.

Green Tea - The first benefit is that it has completely natural ingredients and the second is that there is no caffeine. Your voice's and body will love Green Tea.

Meditation - Keeping your mind even and dealing effectively with stress which is big voice-killer is a great benefit of meditation that will focus your mind and therefore help your singing. Transcendental Meditation is a specific meditation that drops cortisol levels 30% in just one meditation (your stress hormone.) Right away with this technique, the body starts to heal deep stress. It's particularly helpful for anxiety, stress related illnesses, PTSD and heart disease, highly recommended for performers. You'll have a better voice and give better performances as a result.

Chakra work - Besides the benefits of opening the throat chakra, full chakra alignment makes for a healthy body and wellbeing.

Less Acidic Pure Fruit Juices - Drinking fresh, pure fruit juice, such as pineapple, grape and apple juices, help you maintain a high level of energy, and generally help your immune system. Don't drink overly acidic fruit juices such as orange and grapefruit any less than an hour before you're due to sing, as the citric acid can cause excess mucus to develop in your throat.

Voice -killers

'Iced' water - So, you ask for water at the bar and the bar-tender scoops in an avalanche of ice from the ice bucket. This temperature 'shocks' vocal cords!

Dairy Foods - Milk, Cheese and Butter are all foods that tend to cause a lot of mucous; that sticky substance which can interfere a lot when singing. If you must drink milk, follow up with plenty of water to keep your throat clear.

Chocolate - This sublime tasting treat, coats your cords like thick tar and creates a layer of mucus impairing your vocal flexibility. Avoid before you sing. Sad but true!

Alcohol - Alcohol can dry out the throat and cause irritation. It also has a numbing affect which gives you an unrealistic idea of how your voice feels. When you 'can't feel' what's happening with your voice it's not good.

Caffeine - Coffee can dry out the throat, as well as tighten the muscles and restrict vocal range. It de-hydrates, so if you must drink it, follow with plenty of water.

Carbonated or aspartame-containing drinks - These can affect the tone of your voice and increase the amount of air in the stomach.

Acidic Fruit Juice - This can increase the production of mucous in your throat which will get in the way of clear singing.

Stress - Stress is understandably a big voice-killer because when we're in a heightened state of alert, cortisol levels are high in the body and we tend to act from our sub-conscious 'fight or flight' mechanism. Our mind isn't relaxed or focused enough to sing and communicate well because it's focused primarily on survival.

Cigarettes - Cigarettes dry your throat and lungs out and greatly de-hydrate you. It can be said that some good singers have smoked and it didn't appear to be a problem for them. Some even attribute smoking to their 'smoky' vocal tone. In my experience smoking pollutes our voices and lungs causing difficulty with breath control and a higher risk of infections. Besides the obvious life-threatening thing, I've observed over time that all of the people I know of who found nodules on their vocal cords were smokers... even Adele!

In smokers, the lungs weaken and breathing can then become a problem. The ability to breathe correctly is one of the most important attributes a good singer possesses. To hit and hold a high note while singing, a singer must hold deep breaths. A smoker's lungs are likely to have a decreased capability of doing this. If you do smoke make sure to hydrate by drinking plenty of water and if you want to make a positive effort to quit be aware that you'll go through a tricky period for your voice as you give up, as your lungs are rejecting the tar which has accumulated. So you might need a few weeks to re-climatise.

Cannabis - Cannabis burns 100% hotter than tobacco so the smoke is hot, hot, hot and can cause serious damage to your cords in the long term. It will also feel like your voice is on fire, even hotter than your local takeaway's hottest curry dish. You might feel blissfully relaxed for a while but your voice will feel like you've been in a gas chamber for about a week afterwards. How do I know this, you ask? ...Curiosity gets the better of us sometimes, huh? :) If your voice is important to you and as you're reading this it probably is, take care of yourself and give your voice only things that keep it healthy. That way you'll keep it for a long time.

If you find it difficult to relax there are other ways to relax that have only positive after effects which have been scientifically proven. Meditation requires only your intention and it's completely free.

Chapter Eighteen

Chakras

It is said that Chakras are energy centres that are organised along the centre of the meridian points. If a Chakra is out of alignment it is said to be closed or partially closed; not emitting or receiving energy. This can happen due to our body adapting to traumatic experiences. For example, the heart chakra can develop a heart wall to protect itself from receiving further hurt.

Chakras are specific places in the body where we can put our attention in order to unwind any energy blocks in our bodies. They are locations in your subtle, energetic body toward which you can point your attention to experience consciousness more profoundly and with purpose.

Chakras are energy centres in our body and this same understanding has been known for many centuries. Chinese philosophy uses Chakras and the movement of energy as the basis of Acupuncture therapy.

I discovered Chakras through a profound experience. Yes, that's right. You see, I'd been aware of successful singers who take their health very seriously to maximise their performance and many have talked about the importance of Chakras to their health in maximising their potential. So I decided to investigate for myself. I followed some instruction and although I felt a little foolish at first I decided to remain open minded and curious as well as sceptical. Using creative visualisation, I visualised a blue light shining and expanding brighter and brighter in my throat. Within less than a minute something began to happen.

What I felt next I can only describe as a pulsating energy which opened my jaw by reflex and felt like a warm movement of bloodflow which slowly tightened and relaxed muscles in my jaw, my face and up into my scalp in waves that just kept on repeating over and over. I can best describe it as what feels like waves of energy. Nothing else could explain how it feels. It's ever since I first experienced this for myself and that I found I can repeat this phenomena at will that I now confidently include information of their benefits in this book.

In my researching and interviewing people about their experience with Chakras it became clear that other people do experience Chakras slightly differently. Though others could also feel a vibration or pulsation of energy, some experienced little at all except what can only be described as a lighter feeling through unblocking a chakra and what some have described as an internal knowing. Some experienced little at all except what can only be described as a lighter feeling through unblocking a chakra and what some have described as an internal knowing. Don't be too surprised when you feel them though and enjoy the benefits of opening them. When you have opened them for a while it's important to also close them in turn. If you would like to study further into Chakras and their benefits you can find many books and information about them from ancient texts to modern explanations and chakra meditations on the internet.

There are seven key Chakras running up from the base of your spine to the top of your head. These are the Root, Sacral, Solar Plexus, Heart, Throat, Third Eye and Crown. Here are some exercises related to opening the Heart and Throat Chakras:

Heart Chakra - To open your heart Chakra. Place your hands over your heart area. Move your hands in a clock-wise direction around your heart area. Visualise the colour Green or emerald as a vortex of green energy emitting from your heart area.

Surround yourself with green. Eat green foods such as vegetables; Broccoli, lettuce, Spinach, Cabbage. Try Green tea, Sage, Parsley. If you want to you can use essential oils to further stimulate the heart chakra. Essential oils that are associated with the heart chakra are rose, Melisa, Camaomile. Yaro, Neroli and Eucalytus. Minerals or Crystals which stimulate the heart chakra are: Turmeline, Green Cyanite, Rose Quartz, Melocite, Emerald and Jade.

Also practice living from the heart and speaking from the heart. Practice Meta by imagining that your breathing is coming and going from your heart as if breathing in and out from your heart area.

The Throat Chakra is housed in the pit of the throat. Its colour is blue-green and it relates to communication on all levels.When the Throat Chakra is balanced, it brings clear communication and creative expression, from within our self and with others. An open throat chakra lets you express your personal truth and listen more clearly to your inner voice.

Here is a visualisation exercise for your Throat chakra that will help you clear self-doubt and open your personal communication channel. Sit or stand before a mirror. If you choose, you may want to be in front of a bathroom mirror and imagine your daily tooth brushing or mouthwash routine. Except, with this exercise you are going to gargle with an imaginary mouthwash.

Then, close your eyes, focus on your neck and visualise 'blue light' pouring into your throat. Begin to gently hum the letter 'M.' Let the vibration of the letter sound in your throat, creating waves that bathe your throat in blue light.

The Throat Chakra's element is 'ether' and it's considered the "soul's gate," separating our external and internal strengths. The challenge for you working to balance the Throat Chakra is to learn trust in your own voice, find harmony with the world and speak your own truth while trusting your interactions with others in your life.

The Chakras can also respond to specific toned pitches. These Chakra tones are said to correspond in line with 432 Hz rather than commonly used 440Hz western system though many have used C, D, E, F, G, A, B successfully, too instead.

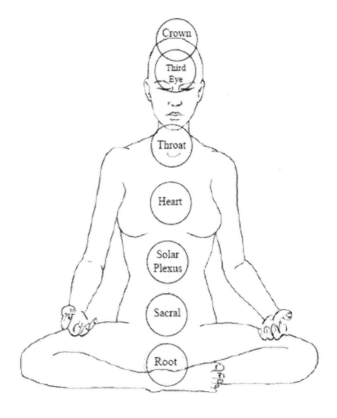

These Chakra tone frequencies are verified by Tibetan Chakra bowls hand-made and played by Monks.

A	Crown	Hz - 216, 432, 864	(Colour Violet)
D	Third Eye	Hz - 144, 288, 576	(Colour Indigo)
G	Throat	Hz - 192, 384, 768	(Colour Blue)
C	Heart	Hz - 128, 256, 512	(Colour Green)
F#	Solar Plexus	Hz - 182, 364, 728	(Colour Yellow)
Eb	Sacral	Hz - 303, 606, 1212	(Colour Orange)
Bb	Root	Hz - 228, 456, 912	(Colour Red)

Whether you explore further into Chakras as means of maximising your vocal health as well as your general health or not it appears that science has finally begun to catch up with proven evidence of the existence of Chakras and this ancient knowledge and how it can sustain and improve your vocal health as many are beginning to experience how this knowledge and practice can envigorate the human body as an open channel to create, express and sing freely.

Good singing in itself is about balance and it appears that in balancing Chakras there is a beneficial affect in singing as well as health and wellbeing. A purveyor to good health is to line up the Chakras and create a good balance of these energy centres.

My following interview with Doctor Laura Koniver, qualified Medical Intuitive will give you more insight into the importance of Chakras both to your singing and your health.

Interview with

Medical Intuitive

Doctor Laura Koniver

Qu: What role do the existence of Chakras play in our health?

I think Chakra flow is so crucial in creative expression of any kind, because the goal of creativity is to be an empty vessel that allows pure spirit and your unique soul energy to flow through you and out to the world. You are the only one who can sing exactly as you sing, just like a painter is the only one who can paint that specific painting and a mother is the only one who can grow that specific child. You are birthing something into this world that no one else can birth when you sing with your unique vocal cords and with your unique soul energy and experience... so the more you can open your body and allow the energy to flow, the better! The more pure and the more potent the effect. So, for that reason, the more open and clear the chakras are, the more powerful your voice can be in that you are closer and closer to expressing pure positive energy direct from source. In this way, ANY chakra can affect the voice depending on the person singing. Although we typically think of the throat chakra as being connected to our voice and inner truth and self-expression through the lungs, any block in any chakra prevents us from being that clear vessel that flows our spirit out and through to the world.

Qu: If Chakras are 'blocked' how does this affect health?

It decreases the flow, simple as that. It just decreases the energetic expression because there is limited flow - it's self-sabotaging. It can create a backup effect on other chakras too -- for example, if the heart chakra is blocked but the throat chakra is open -- the throat can effectively sing a beautiful clear note but it will not be able to flow freely from the heart, so the energy may feel more empty or less *convincing* than one that can freely flow up through the heart chakra and out the throat chakra. All chakras are this way, from crown to root.

Qu: What can we do each day to maintain a healthy Chakra balance?

Open. Open and release. It's all about surrender, that's what I've found out over my past two decades of working in medicine. It's not about what you need to do to correct anything, it's about relaxing into what is already there. Your beautiful unique soul energy is already there. Your own intuitive knowings are already there. Your voice is already within.

Your heart is already beating. Your purpose for being alive on the earth right at this exact moment in time is already a given. The *blocks* we create have to do with our experiences, our traumas, our story about what is going right or wrong at any moment in time.

The most effective way to open and become that vessel of self-expression that any artist/singer is reaching for is just to relax into it. Open, open, open. That's why so many of the most effective techniques at realign health/healing/enlightenment seem so passive -- meditation, transcendental breathing, even sleep is an effective healer as it allows our body to deeply repair and realign. Healing is about relaxing, listening and being present.

It's natural for us to realign with Well Being when we are open to it.

Qu: You made two movies - 'The Grounded,' and 'Heal for free' also known as 'earthing' which reveal the healing power of the earth's electro-magnetic field to reduce inflammation in the body. In vocal health and general health we often resort to pharmaceutical relief or penicillin to combat throat infections and other ailments. What other preventative and natural cures do we overlook?

Like we show in the documentaries you mentioned. Earthing for sure -- that will keep your inflammation constantly resolving and repairing and decrease the over-use injuries that singers can get.

Good hydration -- drink water above and beyond what you think you need to keep your mucosal membranes hydrated. Even using a humidifier in your room at night to sleep in a well moisturized room while you surrender to sleep and repair each night. Fish Oil is great also at keeping your mucosal membranes (and skin) boosted and calm.

Gargling with baking soda and/or apple cider vinegar to help with oral pH... misting your oropharynx with collodial silver at the first onset of any type of respiratory symptom to decrease any URI illnesses that might affect your vocal chords. And energetically, here are a bunch of things you can do for throat chakra support:

(i) Beyond singing ... use your mouth in other ways.

Using your mouth for more than just verbal expression is healthy too! And after you get your mind out of the gutter then you can add all these ways to keep the energy flowing through your throat chakra.

Scream. It's a release and it's fun! Have a screaming contest when you're out with friends or family.

Laugh often. It's fun and it's good for your health! Have a laughing contest when you are out driving with the friends or family.

Yawn — big huge obnoxious yawns… all throughout the day!

Kiss. Groan. Sigh. Stick your tongue out super-far as in the Lion Pose Yoga exercise.

(ii) Journal - Expressing yourself on paper is one of the most cathartic things you can do to release your inner truth.

Many people subscribe to the routine of journaling every day, either through a dream journal, a personal journal, the Artist's Way technique… and even if you are not a routine journaller, writing notes or letters to people that express your inner feelings is a wonderful way to get them out — it's up to you whether you want to send them or not!

One of my families favourite things to do is to write dreams, wishes, desires, or even negative emotions or things we wish to release down on a sheet of paper and then burn them in a bonfire, allowing the energy to release.

Journaling is one of the best ways to invite spontaneous insight, understanding and growth into your life. Journaling is one constant all throughout my Health Flow Unleash course for good reason, because you can dig deep when it's just you and your pen and deeply heal.

(iii) Stop the chatter - Sometimes is it is the absence of noise that allows the space for transformation. Try taking a sabbatical from talking and have a private retreat for a few hours or even a day where you do not talk. Unplug the phone.

Take a break from the near incessant background noise of life by retreating into nature. Spend a day hiking, sleeping on a blanket outside, gardening, walking. Drop the need to be heard and go within.

(iv) Fasting - Along the same lines as a silence retreat, you may find fasting to be a nice way to realign with a fresh start.

Take a weekend to drink plenty of water and perhaps limit yourself to fresh juices or smoothies and let your body take a break from the heavy meals.

Sometimes our mouths do so much processing — between expressing out our words and taking in our food – that giving it a break just feels right.

(v) Deep breathing - Belly breathing provides instant energy flow into your body.

Take one deep breath all the way to the bottom of your stomach right now, and let it out slowly. Don't you instantly notice a feeling of calm, fresh energy flowing through you?

Cultivating a mindfulness breathing practice can help rebalance and restore the flow of your throat chakra in just minutes a day.

Can you recommend a good nutritional diet for Singers?

Throat chakra people just love to enjoy a wide variety of foods and this is one of their wonderful strengths with eating. My son is a throat chakra guy and he is amazing at trying foods most children wouldn't even think of... exotic foods, spicy foods, unusual vegetables that kids traditionally hate. He is open to trying it all and gets so excited as he watches me prepare an interesting meal from scratch. Because they are so open to food, dieting feels like a huge loss and may even bring deep sorrow.

My favorite recommendation for the throat chakra is to focus on trying new and unusual foods to satisfy your cravings, instead of over-eating a large quantity of boring foods. Another great way to look at food for throat chakra peeps is to focus on a Joy Diet! Throat chakra eaters can feel guilty because food brings them joy — but I say this is a strength! Food brings joy! So choose your food selection based on how much joy it brings you and do not waste your time (or calories) on food that does not bring joy.

What greater role can our intuition play in Singing/Performing/life?

I think when we step out of the way and become a vessel for our own unique soul energy to flow through and express, the sound is so much more resonant and infinitely more touching to all the people who hear it. There is a depth and a magical quality that is literally palpable to the listener. I think if you can get into a zone where you are allowing images and feeling and emotions and creative desires to well up from ALL chakra levels and ALL of our current life experiences and ALL of our pain and ALL of our love and ALL of our gratitude -- then you've created something untouchable by anything else. Unreproducible Priceless. My main advice would be to step out of the way as much as possible -- Do not edit any images or emotions or tears or passion or anger or thoughts that flow through you as the voice rings out. You don't know how important these intuitive cellular memories are in self-expression. Even if they don't make sense or are upsetting. Use the energy to pour even more of your soul forth and out into the world. The world is hungry for singers who are fully open, fully alive, and fully willing to share their unique heart song with the rest of the world.

To access more information about Laura's work visit http://www.intuition-physician.com.

I also asked for further clarification on how to make good use of Chakras and received much good advice from Singer, Therapist and Yoga Instructor, Marle Hernandez based in California. Marle advised that you can also make better use of Chakras by exploring each one, understanding how each one relates to health and making time through Chakra meditation to experience each one. While in movement, pause at each chakra and feel each body part it represents. Our bodies retain emotional memory that seeks release. Strengthen each one as you would a muscle. As you would your vocal cords or diaphragm.

Marle also advised that all chakras are equally important in singing because to touch others with the voice is more exquisitely felt and received by them when we are in tune with our bodies.

In relation to Chakras one thing that is most healing for voice care is to take time for yourself. Do things for yourself that make you happy often. Express your feelings out loud in words and learn to communicate with words that convey your heart's truth. Communicate what is important to you and surrender into your own unique expression, freely and clearly.

Part Three

SOUL

"And those who were seen dancing were thought to be insane by those who could not hear the music."

- Friedrich Nietzsche

"Educating the mind without educating the heart is no education at all"

- Aristotle

Chapter One

Define 'Soul'

So, now we enter into a deeper section of our vocal travels. If there were a rabbit-hole section within your vocal exploration then this would be it. Yet, this is the real beauty of it.

The third and arguably the most important ingredient to a Singer's magic formula that gives them that distinctive edge. Your ability to truly express emotion in a song. Your ability to truly communicate the lyric in such a way that completely entrances the listener. In truth if you have 'Soul' sometimes it takes care of the mind and body aspects alone by default.

I asked hundreds to thousands of Singers, musicians and music-lovers 'What do YOU think makes a truly soulful singer?' Here follows a collection of their replies to dwell upon.

Their life experiences expressed to music.
The ability to reach inside themselves.
Communicating the emotion within the lyrics.
To only perform something that they truly feel.
Somebody who makes you believe every single word they are singing...
to the point that you feel as though they can see inside you.
The ability to verbally express any emotion in a song.
Connecting with the emotion, the feeling.
Becoming one with the lyrics and music.
Stage presence.
Their soul's expression.
Honest expression, feelings from the heart.
Sadness expressed as raw, pure emotion.
Body language and facial expression.
Articulating feelings with lyrics.
Both darkness and the light transformed into the beauty of song.
Being able to express themselves emotionally through their voice.

This shortlist may already help stir your imagination towards becoming a more expressive singer. Yet, we must dig deeper to enable you to connect to your own emotions and communicate authentically and convincingly as a Vocal performance.

*"Sam Cooke said this when told he had a beautiful voice: He said, 'Well that's very kind of you, but voices ought not to be measured by how pretty they are. Instead they matter only if they convince you that they are telling the truth.' Think about that the next time you are listening to a singer." - **Bob Dylan***

You may have heard singers described in words such as "they've got soul" or "they're so soulful."

This is where the controversy begins... for some anyway. The 'Soul' of a singer. "Why is this so important?" you may ask. "Are we going to get deeply profound and spiritual from here onwards?"

Well maybe, if that's what you'd like, although it's not my intention to alienate atheist, religious or spiritualist alike because in my humble opinion, either way...we're all in it together. So let's not rule anything out and let's cover all the bases.

I've asked the question, 'What is Soul?' to many successful singers and the answer is always slightly different – It's a very subjective question. Some have taken the question as a purely musical reference whilst others have taken it as a spiritual one. What I've found in time is that both are connected and relevant so however you personally answered, the chances are that you're right. I soon re-phrased the question to 'What is Soul ... to you?' instead. Your own experiences or beliefs will lead you to make your own conclusion but here is some food for thought...

From a strictly cause and effect, 'scientific' basis we can consider 'Soul' as emotion and expression. It's how you as a singer interprets a song in the same way as an actor might portray a part. You've probably heard some people say that 'you either have it or you don't' but let's face it -This very statement is very small-minded.

A singer might not yet feel confident enough in their own skin to fully express a song (yet) but does that mean that they NEVER will? They surely can be led towards it, encouraged to find it and develop it.

If a singer wants to learn to portray more emotion or become more expressive as an artiste there is a process of becoming. Some singers will find this more naturally than others who may at first be more inhibited and that's ok. It's about having the confidence to speak your own truth or express your own personaility within a song idea. Confidence in expressing your own truth.

From another perspective, 'Soul' is expressing something deeper and intangible, sometimes deeply personal or spiritual in nature that can only be attempted to be exposed with words and music. Some will say, 'They've got Soul' as if it's some Jedi technique reserved only for the select few 'special' ones. However, I have seen and heard singers progress and blossom before my own eyes and ears. You could say that singing with 'Soul' is a sort of becoming – a discovery process. As profound as it sounds, it's always quite a transformation. The way that a singer finds their confidence to perform freely and hold nothing back is always to me nothing short of miraculous.

All you have to do is be open to discovery and be prepared to step out of your comfort zone. As you grow in confidence you will let go of your inhibitions and begin to really express yourself through your singing. Let go and become as one with the music. This is pure creativity and expression in action and this is how you can discover yourself as an artiste.

PROCESS - Discover who you are as an Artiste

Step One - Find out 'Who you are' as an artiste. The first step towards becoming a more expressive vocalist is to discover WHO you are as an artiste. You need to figure out how to feel comfortable in your own skin as an artiste.

One thing many Singers agree when I ask them 'What is Soul... to you? is... they often answer 'It's WHO you are' or 'whatever makes you feel ALIVE.' ... 'Whatever personally gives you passion and meaning/ purpose.'

When you really think about it.. How else can a singer truly communicate a song if they don't know how they really FEEL about it? A Singer has to be mindful of how they feel. Have a sense of themselves. And in turn have a true sense of their own values and how they FEEL. You need to make a practice of connecting to these feelings. When you truly FEEL 'it' and communicate your feelings in the music and in your performance, you will have MADE it and FOUND 'who you are' as an artiste.

So, follow this process to getting to know yourself better as an artiste:-

1. Make a list of your favourite songs and artistes. Next, review the list and notice whether they fall into one particular musical style or genre. Do the songs have a similar theme? What story and emotions do they convey? Sing or record a cover of one of these songs.

2. Make a Love/hate list. That's right. There's no point in making a list of anything you feel indifferent or nothing about. What makes you ecstatically happy and what makes you insanely angry or very sad? Extreme emotions also make great songs and inspiring performances. So remind yourself of all of your extreme likes and dislikes.

3. Write down your experiences. Keep a journal or Lyric book and write down your experiences. Not only is this liberating and good self-therapy. It's very creative and will get your creative and emotional juices flowing. What do you need to express and release? Bare your Soul on paper. Tell your unique story. Maybe you'd prefer to record yourself telling the story as audio or video instead and then listen back. If you come across an experience or feeling that is still quite raw, it's an opportunity for you to sink deeper into these feelings, write them down and express them as poetry or song lyrics and release any painful memories in a way that serves you, brings you atonement and perhaps provides an enriched emotional palette of experience that you can draw upon in your singing, as a songwriter and as a performer.

Define 'Soul'

So how can we define singing with 'Soul?' Within your goal of becoming the complete vocalist, soul is an element of great performances that is not easy to define.

First, we're not only talking about the genre of Soul which is a combination of rhythm and blues and gospel, although there is much of what we'll cover in this style of music.

Singing with style can be "taught", but singing with soul is "caught." It's what you feel." - Luv-Luv, American Vocal Coach

Here are some definitions of singing with soul that have been used to describe it.

Singing from the heart
Singing to the heart
Singing with phrasing

Lee Risdale

Singing with expression
Feeling the heart of the music
Creative improvisation

Let's take a look at the benefits of each these and consider how each can create more 'soul' and expression in your performance.

Singing from the heart - Use your own experience. When you're singing the song there may be meaning in the words which resonate with you personally and you are telling this story to your audience. You can make a connection to the feelings you experienced in the present moment as you tell the story as if you are expressing them to a close friend or to the person the song is meant for. You are singing from the heart.

Singing 'to' the heart - Similar to 'Singing from the heart' except you are consoling yourself instead. Perhaps you are coming to terms with a broken relationship or developing inner strength for yourself to get back up from a fall. Maybe you are coming to terms with your feelings. Maybe you are finally able to love or respect yourself 'as you are' without needing any outside approval. All of these are examples of singing to the tune of your own heart.

Singing with phrasing - Ever wondered about where to sing and where not to, how to create pauses and space? How you choose where you sing your notes within the rhythm and pulse of the song can really add more of a dramatic and soulful feel to your performance. Choosing to be creative by singing on off beats and weaving your notes differently within the timing. Chopping up some of the lyric notes and sustaining others for a longer period add more interest and can sound very conversational.

Singing with expression - As an actor conveys feeling within their dialogue, a singer uses similar tool to express their lyric. 'Crying' into your notes or 'crying on pitch' as described in the earlier 'voice qualities' chapter is your prime example. Crying on pitch is an incredible tool which when mastered releases your voice and expresses so much more emotion. However, whether you feel you have mastered cry technique or not, if you can dig deep into the emotive intention of the songs lyric you will communicate this freely and easily. Expression can sometimes also refer to singing with more dynamics which we'll look into later.

Feeling the heart of the music - When you listen to the music on it's own, how does it make you feel? By REALLY listening to the music you're singing with you can create a partnership with it where your voice compliments the music (as the music in turn compliments your voice) So next time you're singing with the music, ask yourself how does it make you feel? The rhythm, the pulse, the groove, the melody. Now absorb these feelings and express them in your singing. You have a partnership with the music.

Creative improvisation - Improvisation is all of the extras you can add in your performance. This can be either within the song lyric or in addition to the lyric which are sometimes known as 'ad libs.' If you're improvising with the song lyric you may be using artistic licence and deviating away from the usual melody line. Therefore the standard melody gets a variation - You can do this rhythmically or in the phrasing by chopping up notes (listen to Jessie J) or sustaining notes too. Adding other embellishments like trills, riffs and runs (see chapter on Style) are also effective improvisation techniques. Ad libs are the extra phrases that can be heard in addition to the song melody structure. They're sometimes heard in the introduction of a song or often in the outro and can be an extension of the lyric, sometimes repeated in a different melody or phrasing.

Listen to 'Heard it through the Grapevine' by Marvin Gaye. At the end, in the outro he sings: "Honey, honey I knooooow. That you'll let me go. Yes, I heard it through the grapevine."

Great Ad lib huh? Marvin's singing a beautiful ascending phrase. What's maybe even greater is that the line is an added lyric, only heard at the end and gives the listener something extra to take away with them.

Singing with Soul

I interviewed many people for their perspective on singing with Soul and here follows some varied and insightful perspectives to inspire you.

"A soulful Singer is someone willing to throw themselves in a state of rawness in front of the world unfiltered. Wanting to make an emotional connection with the listener as if there were the only one, this singer develops intimacy with the whole audience and everyone feels like they are being individually serenaded. Authenticity is the answer." - **Teal Swan, Author and Spiritual Teacher.**

"There is a natural and primitively innate entrainment that occurs with immersion in the timbres, textures and rhythms of music - the waves of tension and release journeying between major and minor. When this entrainment is embraced fully by the singer, and used in cathartic juxtaposition to the life experience, locked within the soul from this quasi-entrancement emerges within the audible carrier wave of sound, the inaudible frequency of the heart - but one which is more profoundly communicable. Something unique to singing - not present in instrumental music" - **Tim Crumper, Musician.**

"What makes a truly soulful singer in that style is there is definitely an element of rawness. The feeling of being 'exposed' and therefore feeling closer to their heart, or their soul for that matter! There is no glossing over going on to try to make the voice sound smooth and good. It is rough edges in the singing that sets of the diamond that is in the form of pure emotion. They are not afraid to go in a channel what they are singing and this fearlessness to diving deep takes us on this journey with them. There

is an element of pain, which gives it its 'soul bearing' quality. So a rock singer can have rough edges, yet this may be from something like anger, but the soul singer has pain that comes from a deep yearning to connect and express." - **Sangetta Lee Jones - Vocalist and Voice Teacher.**

I discovered something. I tried to activate/hold in my Kundalini energy while singing. And WOW it made SUCH a difference - I can now sing with sooooo much emotion. I got the idea from a Kundalini Yoga session, somehow being aware of the Energy Serpent going through the spine, makes you much more connected and grounded. I think singing with authenticity and improvisation whilst being very present in the body are ways to become a great singer - **Linn Aya, Vocalist.**

Singing with soul, to me is the unmasking of hidden overwhelming expressions of you that only sound can extricate. What makes a soulful singer is pouring emotions into every word, allowing the story to move in your voice like a lover's caress. As a singer you can connect to and express your soul, by allowing self-exploration in self-loving acceptance as you are, including and especially what you don't like about yourself, making friends with yourself, falling in love with yourself. Surrendering lovingly into your own voice expression, freely and clearly.
- Marle Angelic Hernandez - Vocalist, Therapist & Yoga Instructor.

"Singers are instruments in themselves that can make all kinds of beautiful music. The music they make is determined by a combination of energies from above and whatever the singer is making of themselves."
Laura LoveMessenger, Author.

"I don't think about what my range is or if I'm keeping my range. It's about... do I feel this? If I can feel it I can hit those notes."
Paul Rodgers, Vocalist.

More than anything else be brave and bold enough to express your own personality in your singing. Your own unique personality and experience of the world offers a unique perspective that will be heard in your singing. This authentic, raw truth is what your audience secretly long to hear and it's how you can truly make a connection with your listener.

Chapter Two

The Singing Actor

Singing may require some acting ability too. Take the showmanship performances of Freddie Mercury or David Bowie, Madonna or Beyonce which are very theatrical. Some actors can also make great singers and if not they can often compensate for lower vocal ability with their 'acting' because so much of good singing is in the expression.

If you are new to performing to an audience or you're a low confidence singer you can find much confidence in assuming another persona in the same way that an actor assumes a character. Assuming a role in this way can bring a confidence to a singer that that they may otherwise struggle to find or achieve only after years of experience.

Actors draw upon various techniques. One well known example is 'method acting' which was pioneered by Constantin Stanislavski and later adapted by Lee Strasberg. This involves connecting to a character by drawing on personal emotions or memories and simulating their behaviour by 'acting out' based on the character's motivation.

Whatever is the character role, the actor can sometimes spend days or weeks 'becoming' that character both in their attitude and their actions.

So have a think about what you want to convey or portray on stage in your performance and list all these things on a piece of paper. You may want to list them in respect to individual songs.

Here are some questions you can ask yourself based on your motivation to 'act out' and truly express the song. Answer these questions with respect to a particular song or musical theme. They will help you to develop your interpretation.

What is the song about?
What are the lyrics saying?
Are the lyrics happy, positive, sad, melancholy, angry, bitter, passionate?
What is the core meaning or feeling throughout the song?
What dynamics (energetic high points, low points) are within the song?
How can you express these lyrics effectively to your audience?

Think about the overall theme of the song. As the communicator of this song...

What attitude will you portray?
How will this affect your posture onstage?
How will this motivation affect your facial expression?
How does your character truly feel?
How does the song truly make you feel?

When I began as lead singer in a Soul band we played many challenging classic Soul songs from the likes of Sam Cooke, Otis Redding, James Brown, Marvin Gaye and Al Green to name a few. The prospect of singing these classic songs and attempting to communicate and express the spirit of these great artistes would have been intimidating to any young caucassian singer. Besides this there was some doubt from others that as I didn't possess the genes of an African American. Therefore, in their opinion, I was disadvantaged. Dis-illusioned at best.

But these amazing singers and artistes were my idols and was determined to give it my best. I started by playing the music on repeat, over and over and I allowed the Soul of the music to soak into my very being. Great music, so that part was easy. Next I listened to live performances and watched archived footage. I observed not only the expression of the artistes but how they carried themselves in their posture. How they interacted with their audience. How they moved onstage. They became my greatest teachers.

I listened to how Otis would passionately punch out his lyrics with explosive articulation. I watched him stomp across the stage with relentless energy, an unstoppable force. I listened to Sam Cooke's smooth vocal delivery and how he could sing raucously too as he completely charmed his audience to their feet. I listened to Marvin Gaye's dynamic range and the way he could sing both with sensual expression one moment and the next, sing with such passionate pleading. I listened to James Brown's fire-filled vocal tone and rhythmic phrasing which he could blend into a soulful rasp in his ballads. I watched him shuffle and slide across the stage like nobody else.

Then I went about taking all I had learned from them and applied it in our band performances. The result of this for me became years of repeat bookings. Many gigs and very excited audiences. I had learned my craft...I had become a Singing actor of sorts, imparting the true spirit of Soul music - and it was a LOT of fun!

An element of acting can be a really good thing that can truly enhance your performance. To do it well you must immerse yourself in the part, the motivation and the attitude of the music. If you only take one or two ideas from the performance of an artiste you respect and bring them into what you do, you will be adding a new dimension to your performance.

That's not to take away anything from what you do already. Think of it this way. Every single artiste learns something from another artiste. This has always, always been the case. Mahalia Jackson influenced

Little Richard who influenced Otis Redding and also James Brown. James Brown influenced Prince and Michael Jackson who influence... countless people.

You don't have to copy an artiste entirely like a tribute artist, although I know many singers who make a respectable living doing just that. You simply take influence of the things you like and include it in your performance. The result of your interpretation will come across differently anyway because you are a unique individual. But these ideas taken and adapted can greatly enhance what you do. Think of it as adding yet another delicious flavour to the amazing cocktail of your performance!

"I am the king of re-invention" - Bob Dylan

If you are a singer who seeks only to write your own songs and be completely authentic in your expression of those songs (as you wrote them - expressing them should be easy, right?) there will still always be something invaluable to learn from listening to or watching another artiste perform that can subtly but positively affect your own performance.

After all, a great deal of great vocal performances ... contain a high element of acting!

Chapter Three

Express the Intention of the Author

In this section we're going to tackle how to sing a cover of someone elses's song by really understanding the lyric. We need to understand or at least identify with the intention of the author so we can sing it convincingly. So how do you make an audience believe every word you're singing...?

First, we need to delve further into your imagination in respect of the song itself and the lyrics. Interpretation is a word that often arises when working on performances. Interpretation is about 'expressing the intention of the author.'

This means that you're going to examine the song text or lyrical content of your song and use your own creativity to truly magnify, illustrate and express the back-story of the song in your performance. We're finding out your own personal take on the story of the lyrics. This is a subjective exercise and I invite you to use your imagination.

Let's begin by asking a few questions...

Where and when is the back-story of your song taking place?
Has it taken place in the past, is it in the present or future?
Can you visualise where it's happening?
Who is involved in the story?

Can you relate the lyrics to your own experience? Joy...longing, heartbreak...?

Print or write out a copy of your lyrics. Take a pencil and jot some notes against key words or phrases. Sometimes you can add specific expressions or voice qualities to emphasise some words. Use your own intuition to highlight what rings true for you. What we're doing here is delving deeper into the lyrics and their meaning to enable you to truly understand the song. True understanding of the song and most importantly, how you feel about it is what's important here.

If you feel nothing about the lyric and you feel indifferent it might be wise NOT to sing it. Wherever possible, sing only songs that you can truly feel and identify with in some way. As another option, put your acting hat on and refer to our previous chapter.

Perhaps you can empathise or relate in some way to a song or role to pull it off but there's nothing quite as good as interpreting and expressing a song that you relate to from your own personal experience. We've all heard songs that affect and touch us deeply that we can truly relate to and when you really think about it, these are the songs that we ought to be singing. Someone once told me, "If you don't feel it, don't sing it!" Go water the garden instead. Or go out and live that experience for yourself to draw upon a richer palette of feelings. After all, life is for living. Then oneday you will find you have the emotional intelligence backed up by experience to sing many more songs.

If you can't feel it ... Don't sing it!

Imagination and visualisation are the key here when Expressing the intention of the author. So ask yourself:

1. What is the song about?

2. What does it really mean to me?

3. Is there a specific mood running through the song? Can I name it?

4. Are there high and low points, dynamically? If so, where are they?

5. Are there specific words or phrases that need singing differently? If so, which ones?

As you answer these questions in relation to your chosen song, begin to think about more voice qualities and how you can adapt your voice quality and volume level to suit various sections of the song.

Will you begin softly in a breathy falsetto quality? Will you begin in 'speech quality?' Will you lift your volume level in the bridge section? Perhaps you will 'Belt' or 'Mixed Belt' into the Chorus or even add a raspy edge. If a line is deeply emotive 'cry' into the lyrics.

Think carefully about where in the lyrics you can use different voice qualities effectively to add drama and dynamics to the lyric and mark any changes in dynamic quality and volume level choices clearly on your lyric sheet (more on dynamics later).

There might be some stylistic complications with a song you're attempting to sing. You wouldn't expect Rod Stewart to sing Nessun Dorma by Pavorotti. Pavorotti might have struggled to interpret 'Do you think I'm sexy?" or "Maggie May." By the way, don't try to imagine this...damn, too late! :) Use your own feelings and intuition to guide you with stylistic choices and wherever possible, stylstically adapt a song to fit your own style of singing.

There is such an art to stylistically changing a song but keeping the intention of the lyric convincing and this is truly where your own personal take on the song lyric can really shine through because a song can be expressed almost entirely differently by another artiste, depending on their own personal understanding and expression of it.

Doing it 'your way' or 'I did it my way' to quote Frank Sinatra wouldn't be possible without understanding the lyric and what that lyrical intention means to you. If you're not someone who makes notes on lyric sheets and you prefer to simply experiment with this, listen to the song on repeat several times until you get a really good idea how you feel about it. Press your thumb and forefinger together as you listen and allow yourself to feel those feelings. This will help to 'anchor them in' to your subconscious and when it comes to performing the song you can access that same feeling again simply by pressing your thumb and forefinger together. Try this as an experiment.

This is you, telling the story of the song in your own style. So express your version of the story. Tell the story as no-one else can because no-one else can tell it quite like you can. This is story-telling in its most expressive form. In a song to music. How will YOU express the story?

Singers who truly express the back-story of the songs lyric give very authentic powerful performances. You can do this too by simply learning your lyrics well and committing to telling that story as though you're telling it for the first time - every time! Your way.

It's not surprising that singers who don't learn their lyrics well sing with a real lack of conviction. They haven't understood the lyric and so they can't really communicate the song. Take the time to understand your lyric and you'll not only be able to express it well... You'll sing it with conviction!

Continuing with our theme of Expressing the Intention of the Author, interpretation and considering the motivation from a Singing actor's perspective, I interviewed Singer and Voice-over artiste Rosalind Morena-Parra to share perspective from her experience.

Interview with

Singer & Voiceover Artist

Rosalind Moreno-Parra

Qu: How and why did you get into singing?

"Singing for me was influenced by playing the piano and experimenting with creating music and writing songs. Essentially, I wanted to sing the music I was writing and tell stories through music. I think I was influenced by earlier experiences of being in Spain with my family, (my mother is Spanish) and seeing female members of my family singing at parties and cultural fiestas. I remember feeling inspired by that. I used to sing when I was little because I wanted to emulate these women. I was brought up in England, so for me it was like a connection to Spain and my Spanish roots. I think that's what started me singing. Then because teachers picked up on my singing, I did a lot of theatre productions and Drama at school. I've always sung since then and been in bands of various kinds. More recently I've come back to that original thing that got me into singing, - wanting to tell my tales through music."

Rosalind writes and performs her own music in Bristol and covers some traditional Ladino and Spanish singers too. She has become a popular main act at many Spanish and Tango nights as well as at various events in the UK. She performs accompanied by her acoustic guitarist, violinist and cajon player. She also plays piano beautifully on some of the songs. The music is perfect for dancers. It's deeply romantic and passionate and has her audience spellbound with her rich tone and vibrato as she sings lyrics entirely in Spanish. There is something hypnotic about the music and the sound of the Spanish enunciation which I remember from my childhood holidays in Spain. It's surprising that regardless of her fluent singing in Spanish, hearing Rosalind speak she has a well-articulated English accent. She previously was lead vocalist for Hispanic-influenced touring band Sufira, who have played many UK festivals and she has experience of singing many other styles, including Jazz. She has great talent and works as a Voiceover artist and has done much work for the BBC.

"The reason I got into singing was somewhat different for me when I started ....then it was about freedom - I saw freedom in singing. I saw a rich palette of expression and emotion which I was really craving when I was little. Now, for me it's the biggest stress reliever and it's a way I can feel really empowered and alive. It's also a way of celebrating what's good in life as well as dealing with my shadows. Sometimes I write and

Lee Risdale

*perform music that connects me with the deepest and darkest things...
things that are easiest for me to process by singing or sometimes even
howling about them! Sometimes I sing ancient songs which remind me
of where I came from and keep me feeling connected to Spain and my
lineage... It's the biggest thing that helps me feel joy and to feel alive and
confident. I create connections with people through singing that I can't in
any other way, such as with dancers – creative connections with people
'in the moment, observing the magic that happens spontaneously.."*

**Qu: Do you have a routine that you do to prepare yourself mentally
or physically to perform?**

*"At University I did loads of singing in big productions where I'd
experience a lot more nervousness . I had to remember hundreds of
lines of dialogue aswell as singing big numbers with huge range. To
manage this, I had to do a lot of breathing work and I remember having
a few drinks sometimes before going onstage! I used to drink Red wine
and Port which would warm my throat. When I did big gigs later on with
Sufira in London I would do things to manage any anxiety I had... I'd
do lots of physically 'grounding' my body and then I would visualise.
I would remember when we won part of the Glastonbury new talent
competition or I'd hold an image of a performance that we'd done
somewhere really special that went really well. I'd think about that and
have that in my head. Visualising like that, always puts me in touch with
what I wnated to CREATE and have happen... I would remember how
a gig went really well or the images of the crowd ... of how alive and
happy they looked. So sometimes it's holding an image of something
that went really well and sometimes it's about acceptance. I have high
expectations of myself which can cause stress, so I have a little mantra
about being 'good enough.' Some mantras or affirmations that I say that
help with any performance anxiety include: 'Great things will happen
this evening' or 'I'm a GOOD ENOUGH singer. Also, I remind myself
that things that bring me great joy are not always perfect. I've seen
amazing performances where things go wrong,*

*-people dropped the mic, a piece of equipment broke, or someone's voice
cracked up halfway through,- but that's not the part that you remember.
It's HOW ALIVE someone is when they sing to you or how connected they*

are to their music. So I remind myself of those things and that usually grounds me enough to walk out in front of big audiences.

Qu: Have you always been a confident singer? What did you do to develop your confidence?

"I think I had a lot of encouragement from my parents to sing. I haven't always been a confident singer because there is a point you get to where you're singing either as an amateur or professional. If you mix with other people that you feel can REALLY SING, suddenly you feel like you CAN'T sing (Comparing) and that's where the acceptance comes in. To manage this I say to myself: Ok, I'm not an extraordinary singer with a really amazing voice but I LOVE singing and it makes me feel truly alive and I want to share that with everyone... and hey it's not so bad if people don't enjoy it,- I can accept that. In fact people get a lot from it in spite of whether it's phenomenal or not. I remind myself that it's the experience that matters. **What helps me still go out there?** *I had a studio voice job to do once that was really daunting. This client wanted me to recreate something another brilliant singer had already recorded but asked me to improve on it. He played the recording and the singer had an incredibly athletic voice and huge range and held one note for what seemed to be to be about 30 seconds. There was a moment there when I had a crisis of confidence. "Why me?", I thought. "I can't improve on this, this singer is phenomenal!". I still had to do it. I could have walked way but I chose to do it. I said to the client: "Why do you want **me** to do this?" when this singer has such an amazing voice and he said the orginal didn't sound sad enough. I thought maybe he's going to hear this again later and just go with the great voice, or maybe not. Maybe what I can give him is not amazing but it's something unique that will be of use to him. So I now remember that 'Good enough' is 'good ENOUGH.' One thing that gives me confidence now is that I remember I'm not perfect but I have uniqueness in what I do. I mean, you might listen to a singer like Tom Waits and you might not think he has such a great voice but It's not just about the quality and perfection of someone's voice - It's about what you FEEL when you're in their presence. It can be about what you connect to in their eyes when they sing. I also remember that it doesn't HAVE to please everybody. This is something I do because I love it. If some people get something from it then that's GREAT... and if other people don't but I'm doing something that I LOVE it's good for me, you know? It's a bit*

like someone who goes running. They might not be a great athlete or be running a marathon but they know that it's good for them... or it feels good. In saying that - we are social beings. If nobody appreciated my music it would be harder...an appreciative audience does make it easier. But I think you can be closed to the positive things people are saying and focusing on what wasn't right with the performance. So it's also about really acknowledging when people say something positive. Now when people say something positive, I really try to think about what they've said and savour it, because wow! that was their experience.

I also think it helps to be willing to make yourself vulnerable. To create intimacy and relate to people you have to be prepared to allow yourself to be vulnerable. Vulnerability enables people to connect to you as a performer. Allowing yourself to be who you are, is far preferable to emulating someone else who you might admire. If you idolise a singer because you think they have strength... and many do this, try also to find that strength within yourself as well, because you have it too. It may take you longer to recognise it or you may still be in the process of finding it, but you will"

Rosalind and I discussed and agreed on this point: If you idolise or desire to emulate another singer, what you're looking at is a mirror of what you desire yourself. You would be wise to develop and nurture these qualities within yourself. "*If you spot it, you've got it!*" Rosalind says.. "*the qualities are already there waiting for you to find them.*"

Qu: What skills make a good Voiceover Artist?

"*Determination.You need determination to survive in this industry. It takes determination to get a Voiceover agent initially and to remain busy in that world is difficult because you're freelancing a lot so you've got to keep putting yourself out there and selling yourself. Some technical information and understanding is useful. So, for example learning to understand and work with time codes is really important for studio work. Also you need to become flexible and adept at adapting your voice on the spot. In this vein being versatile is important and getting good at taking direction. Have a good sense of listening out for what the client REALLY wants because there's often too much information or direction which is almost impossible to remember, so you have to whittle it down to the key area of what's important for the client. Practical skills involved include good mic technique and voice control using the breath. Learn which positions to the mic create the vocal sound someone is looking for. Eg. The closer to the mic you get the more intimate your voiceover will sound.*

Qu: Do you prefer to sing in English or Spanish?

"I used to prefer singing my own songs in Spanish and it's quite nice that a lot of people who aren't fluent in Spanish don't understand what I'm singing about ." (Laughter,- I could see the benefits in this.) *"There's a certain level of privacy when singing my own songs in Spanish, especially the deeper, personal stuff that renders you more vulnerable... Overall I think I prefer singing in Spanish or Ladino. I think for me singing is integral to me expressing who I am in the world. I suppose the types of music I sing, such as Ladino or Tango music, allow me more freedom to express myself. They are styles that are quite free vocally. I sing between the tones, semitones and quarter-tones as in much Indian music. When I write in these styles it helps me to really connect with the music expressively. Lots of my Spanish songs have a lot more words in, so if I translate them to English text I have to simplify them a lot to make them work. At the moment I'm enjoying singing more in Spanish but it really changes a lot and changes with my mood."*

Qu: What's important to you for vocal Health? How do you take care of your voice?

"I've had to take a lot of care, especially as a Voiceover artist. No smoking, no dairy before voice work as it makes your voice really sticky and inflexible. On the day or night before a voice-over job I try not to do any loud shouting and I drink lots of water. On the day, I take something with me like Glycerine (a voice moisturiser)."

Qu: What is singing with 'soul' to you?

Soul to me is the essence of who you really are. It's that sense of real aliveness, that part of you that's really connected, alive and vibrant in the moment. It's a bit like what Drama schools teach in relation to 'method acting', but using your voice. When you connect to an experience you've had that's similar to what you are wanting to convey, that enables you to perform more authentically. You connect to an experience that really means something to you and it helps you tell your vocal story in a way that is believable.

Qu: Is there a fine line between 'singing acting' and really expressing your own song with conviction?

"Singing my own material always feels different. For me the difference is comparable to when you're acting and either using a script or performing your own material...there's a whole lot less acting when you're performing your own material. There's a real difference in how vulnerable you feel if you're singing your own songs rather than covers. If you expose your own feelings and using your own words, it's just you and the audience and nothing between your mind and theirs. I like to write in 'metaphors' because it's far less emotionally raw and sometimes quite protective in terms of what you are disclosing about yourself to an audience. If you're singing covers you can still bring yourself to the material though, interpreting it in your own style. Sometimes when we sing covers we may have to represent a specific style and this is much more like acting, becoming another person or stepping into another world. I used to sing in a Jazz band that felt a lot like this. It can be good to keep a balance between the two to keep the style or flavour but add your own interpretation and improvise."

Listen to Rosalind's beautiful music at http://www. rosalindmorenoparra.com

Chapter Four

Getting into the Zone

I encounter this often with singers. Many singers sometimes struggle to sing a song from that place where they're living, breathing, singing their song as if they're feeling all of the emotions right here... in the present moment. Some singers can walk through the door and get into that place everytime while many others just have no idea how to do that. It's usually because the song is new to them, they're still unfamiliar with it so they're not expressing it and sometimes they're self -conscious about 'feeling it' before an audience.They're more concerned with 'singing it right' It's admirable to care about singing it well but the truth is that all of that can take place in your rehearsal.

If you learn to sing a song well enough by rehearsing it well, when it comes to the performance, it's more about really 'feeling it' and convincing the audience that you mean it. Don't be afraid to go to that place because the audience will love you for it. Nothing is more attractive to the listener than a singer who truly authentically feels the song and their communicating it enables the listener feel it too by default.

This is often referred to as 'getting into the zone.' It's about drawing upon your feelings without hesitation during your singing and expressing them clearly in your performance.

Many singers get nervous before they perform. Their 'fight or flight' mechanism kicks in and it seems they have no hope of even glimpsing 'the zone.' How can they, when their whole body is screaming 'red alert!?' Refer to the earlier 'Mind' section of this book for techniques on handling fear.

'Getting in the zone' may be new to you though so here are some useful techniques to try to help you 'get into the zone.'

1. Close your eyes. That's right. Your sight sense is redundant here because all you really want to be focusing on is the song, your memorised lyrics, the music... and most importantly 'how you feel' about it. Closing your eyes, if only for certain moments in the songs provides a sensual deprivation that focuses your attention fully on the song and the emotion. Sometimes you will have seen singer/songwriters keeping their eyes closed throughout the whole song or even their entire performance (and I'm not just talking about the magical Stevie Wonder or Ray Charles although with these great artistes I can rest my case entirely!).

So close your eyes, allow yourself to feel the music and the intention of your song lyric. Allow yourself to become immersed in the music and all of the feelings that it brings up for you...and you WILL communicate that song!

2. Take a really slow, DEEP breath. This helps to calm and reassure your body and really takes the edge off of any nerves. Spiritual practices such as Yoga and Meditation teach the benefits of low diaphramatic breathing for a deeper connection, good health and wellbeing. There is absolutely something very magical and confidence building about breathing this

way that fully connects a singer to their own unique power and it will help you get into the zone.

3. Lower your brain frequency. 'What...?' I hear you say. 'How the hell am I going to do that!?'

I'll tell you. There are four distinct levels of brain frequency that can be measured. Beta, which is wide awake. Alpha, which is a bit like day-dreaming, Theta, which is a sleepy, dreamy, deep meditation state and Delta, when you're fully asleep.

It's actually quite easy to access Alpha state and very natural with practice. One way is simply to de-focus your vision. So, if you've ever been in that 'day-dream' state where you 'zone out' when you maybe should have been concentrating but your mind wanders elsewhere... THAT is alpha state where you have the choice to embed ideas, feelings and information in your sub-conscious mind.

All you have to do is relax, de-focus your vision slightly (which you might remember feels a bit like staring into space) and let your mind wander off straight into your song and all of the feelings that this brings up for you.

Just allow the feelings to wash over you as you sing each line of your song. You might want to listen to the song in this mind state first. Then, once you've rehearsed the lyrics, melody and phrasing well enough so that you're really familiar with the song it will be easy for you to focus purely on anchoring these points of reference (the feelings) so that you can recall and express these feelings naturally with the song when you perform it.

4. Understand your lyric. This goes back to our last chapter 'expressing the intention of the author.' If you know your song well and understand the meaning of the lyric and how YOU feel about it, this will again help you in 'getting into the zone' because your understanding of the song will practically be woven into your DNA. When you truly understand a song it's almost impossible not to express it so it's Win Win!

Lee Risdale

Like many of the techniques in this book try to make a habit of practicing and applying them often and notice how your singing begins to feel more natural and flow. Also notice how your audience respond positively to your performance.

Chapter Five

Singing with Dynamics

Dynamics are softness and loudness - volume levels. As a song can have changes in dynamics from verse/bridge/chorus/middle eight, you can express these changes and moods as portrayed from the lyric. When you add good vocal dynamics you add much more interest to your singing. Otherwise singing at the same volume level is quite boring. So figure out where you can include dynamic changes. It may help you to choose and mark your own dynamic changes on a lyric sheet. Here's an example using volume and voice qualities (return to Section 2, the Body for explanation on voice qualities);

Verse: Softly/breathy tone
Bridge: Medium loud/speech quality
Chorus: Loud/mixed, belt
Middle 8: Falsetto/speech with crescendo

Chorus: Loud/mixed belt

Naturally not all songs will require you to sing with so many dynamic changes but be creative and mindful of where you can introduce them to great effect.

Here are common dynamic markings as can be found in a musical score. These will direct you if you're singing a cover from a lead sheet.

pp - pianissimo - (Very Softly, gently)
p - piano (Soft, gently)
mp -mezzo piano (Medium Soft)
mf - mezzo forte (Medium Loud)
f - forte (Loud)
ff - Fortissimo (Very Loud)

Further common dynamic markings and techniques include:

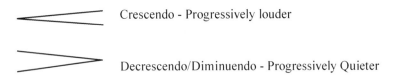

Crescendo - Progressively louder

Decrescendo/Diminuendo - Progressively Quieter

Sing Crescendo

If you want to create a crescendo effect the emphasis is on breath control. Let's examine the basic mechanics of Crescendo.

1. Supplying a column of air using your diaphragm.
2. Making tone by vibration of vocal folds in resistance to airflow.
3. Increasing the airflow pressure gradually against thicker vocal folds.

So, the question is, how do we increase the pressure? If you're shouting out to someone in another room in the place where you live and you instinctively raise your voice it's a very natural thing to do. A crescendo is a gradual increase in volume though. Besides your diaphragm itself, our abdominal muscles further engage. The abdominal wall is attached to your pelvic diaphragm which also acts to increase pressure. Think of the diaphragm the pelvic diaphragm as two balancing hands. Your diaphragm acts as a steady pump of airflow, whilst your abs and pelvic floor work to increase the airflow. As you relax your diaphragm as your exhale, the airflow also increases. You then lean in with your cords to provide more resistance to this increase in airflow which then creates more volume. The reverse then creates less volume.

Muscles of forced expiration:

1. The Pelvic diaphragm a.k.a. the pelvic floor muscle (lower pelvis)
2. Abdominal wall.
3. Epigastrium (below your sternum/at the top of the abdominal wall).

Exercise One - Sing three separate notes at the same pitch in stocatto. Now engage your abdominal muscles more inensely on each sucessive note so that the second note is slightly louder than the first and the third note is the loudest. Your Epigastrium muscle provides a kick and pelvic diaphragm reinforces support. As you do this ddd more cord closure, leaning in with cords. Now try this same exercise with different vowells.

Exercise Two - Repeat the previous exercise except this time use an 'Nng' tool to encourage tone and sustain/hold the three notes incrementally at the same pitch. Increase your volume on each notes as before so that the third note is the loudest.

Exercise Three - Repeat the exercise but this time sing 'Ah' as just one long sustained note. Gradually and progressively increase your volume (Crescendo) over a count of 4 or 8 and try this on various pitches starting from low to high. Aim to increase your volume very gradually, increasing your volume smoothly with control.

Sing Decrescendo

The three previous exercises work the same except in reverse. Try them again but this time focus on starting louder and the third note or end of phrase will be softer and quieter in volume. Reducing airflow gradually can be quite difficult to master and you'll need to carefully use the same support muscles in reverse. You can subtly reduce your cord closure to also achieve the effect of softening the tone to blend into lower volume.

Messa Di Voce

Contemporary Speech Level Singing vocal training derived partly from traditional Italian Bel Canto singing which has existed for centuries. Here is a Bel Canto technique and exercise designed for you to develop your dynamic control. Messa Di Voce pronounced Messa Di Voi-che is the principle of developing greater dynamic control in singing crescendo and decrescendo. As we know, it can be dull to hold one note at the same volume level for longer than a few seconds so some dynamic change is desirable to keep your listener engaged.

Exercise One:

Sing "Ah - Oo" three times on one pitch building to crescendo with "Ah" and receding in decrescendo on "Oo," taking a breath between these three stages. Hold "Ah" for four seconds before changing to "Oo" vowell.

1) Full Voice (Ah-Oo).
2) Half Voice (Ah-Oo).
3) Falsetto, Breathy/Low volume (Ah-Oo).

Exercise Two:

Now try this again, singing "Ah-Oo" as you ascend pitch upwards by a fourth interval on "Oo" on the second note to these pitches on a piano. You may find it easier to do this by putting a 'G' or an 'M' consonant before the vowell at first. Then try it singing the pure vowells without the aid of the consonants. When you feel you've mastered this, try Messa Di Voce with song phrases you're familiar with.

Ab - Db (Ah- Oo)
A - D (Ah- Oo)
Bb - Eb (Ah- Oo)

And now these:

B - E (Ah- Oo)
C - F (Ah- Oo)
Db - Gb (Ah- Oo)
D - G (Ah- Oo)

Other great ways to add further dynamics and expression into your singing are:

Accents - Accents are emphasising a particular note or phrase with more energy than previous notes. Accents can be short, articualted notes and this can be really effective to emphasise an really emotive part of your song.

Changing Voice Qualities - As in Section Two where we looked at voice qualities, experiment with using various qualities during the song. Examples of qualities you can switch between and combine are: Speech, Cry, Twang, Mix, Belt, Rasp and Falsetto (see Voice Qualities).

Speech is the most common quality used in Pop music. Twang can be used to project your tone more distinctly and is used in many styles from Jazz to Rock to Musical Theatre. Cry has that raw emotive quality that translate passion in any genre of music. Mix adds intensity and Belt or Mixed Belt projects power and energy. Rasp and Vocal fry are really effective in bringing grit and rawness to a performance.

Falsetto is the breathy quality that expresses a light and subtle yet beautiful contrast to the heavier voice qualities. It has be almost used like a whisper (a lot of airflow, cords vibrating on their very edges only) which can be really effective when recorded.

Experiment with interchanging between these voice qualities or combining them and take time to figure out where to use each in your song. As you get into the habit of practicing them regularly you'll develop a broad pallette of choices that you can improvise with during any song you sing. Be experimental and take risks with this. Notice how some of your favourite singers adapt and combine voice qualities in their performances. Speech quality is a good home base to return to and is neutral. Your pure tone. But this living on the edge in experimenting with dynamic voice qualities will make your singing far more exciting.

The fun thing about dynamics are the choices you make which are unique to you and the songs you're singing. You don't have to sing a song exactly like another singer or as the original. Dynamics are another creative way of making it your own. So if it feels good, take some risks!

Chapter Six

Relating to your Audience

You may have heard how singers seem to relate to their audience effortlessly. They appear confident and they always seem to know how to address an audience and how to bring them onside and draw them to both themselves as an artiste and as a performer.

If you're a less confident or slightly shy performer this can be intimidating because you're still figuring out how to appear and how to perform confidently, You might be daunted by what is in a sense, public speaking even if it's in a casual musical performance.

When your audience is happy, your singing, the band performance, everything just flows so much easier. There is no scrutiny or hang-ups about absolute musical perfection because... you've already won! They're in the palm of your hand and you can do no wrong. They're dancing, moshing, rocking, swaying (classical) or whatever feels good because you've charmed them or at least created a common ground so they're on your side.

So how do you 'Get the audience?' Surely this is something that a singer needs to learn to do. How do you create the right atmosphere that enables them to relax, lose all their inhibitions and surrender completely to your music?

Ok, well I have to say that just when you think you've figured it all out, there will sometime be an audience you just can't win over. Maybe you can't win them all...But, here are some great techniques that can win an audience over.

1. Greet your audience - Nothing warms up a chilly audience more than a greeting that sets the tone for your performance. You can choose when you greet them but usually when you enter the stage or after the first song is good. HOW you greet them is your choice and all you have to do is greet them in a way that best fits with the music and the event. So a respectful and gracious introduction might suit a Classical music event while a string of four letter words might suit a Punk gig perfectly and create just the right energy to kickstart the performance. Some bands feel that saying nothing or acting un-interested is cool in some way but my experience of this is that it creates a wall between you and the audience which gets in the way of them feeling part of your performance and interacting with you. Greet them with enthusiasm because your audience want to feel that they made a great choice by being there with you.

2. Introduce members of the band - This is actually a really effective way of warming the audience to your band. Introduce them by name and the instrument they play. You can do this early in the set or you choose one player at atime in-between each song to introduce. Another way is to have a song which each of your band members play a solo and introduce them for their solo. This can create a real buzz for the band and overall unity in the performance, too.

3. Tell them the background of a Song - It can add more meaning to a performance when you sometimes explain the background of a song, why, where or when it was written. Learning the background of a song involves the audience more, especially if they relate to the back-story. You can even begin 'have you ever been in this situation when....' scenario as befits the song which can immediate help them to relate to you and the song in question. If it's a cover, some background on the original writer or artiste is good too, because it can add some interest and trivia. It also shows your respect for the origins of the music.

4. Call and response singing - This is maybe one of the best ways to pull in your audience and get them interacting with you. It's quite simple, really. You let them know, you're going to sing a line and you want them to sing it back to you. Create space in the music to do this and improvise. Keep the phrase you sing simple, rhythmic and melodic. You can rehearse where you might use this within your song or within your setlist. When I began using this with my band it practically lifted the whole audience response so much that I began using it all of the time. You don't have to be Freddie Mercury or Aretha Franklin to pull this off (although it's true that this level of conviction might help). Audiences usually love to sing and will take an opportunity to sing with you during your performance using call and response. Sometimes the more urgency and demanding tone you imply with your audience, the better they respond. You might find that later in your set, if not at the beginning, you'll only have to sing a phrase and point your microphone towards them and they'll be chanting every word back to you. In fact, I can testify that they will. If you can get them singing with you, you've got them!

5. Tell them what you want them to do - There is nothing quite like the power of a microphone that is amplified for convincing an audience to do whatever it is you want them to do. The hypnotic effect of the music in itself combined with the rhythm of your voice is often hypnotising in itself. In fact, 'hypnotic language' is a method of using the rhythm and the pitch of your voice in various ways to get required responses and this is something that you can research further if you'd like. There is something about a relatively high spoken pitch descending to a low pitch that gives a command with conviction in the spirit of participation.

So if you want your audience to sing, tell them. If you want them to dance, tell them. If you want them to dance on the tables, tell them. You can use the word 'please' if you like but it won't be necessary. In fact the more you command it they won't be able to resist. Your audience ultimately want to have a great time... So give them a great time! They're going to have fun, whether they like it or not. Otherwise, they might as well stay at home and watch some other people having fun on TV. If the music is good, usually your audience don't even need to be told or asked. I've seen some crazy stuff! Sometimes your audience might need more persuading or it might be that your music speaks for itself and you don't feel you need to do this but try this... and you will be surprised how effective it is. Your audience will love you for it.

Chapter Seven

Stage Prescence

You might have heard the phrase 'stage prescence' mentioned if you've been involved in music performance or watched other bands and singers perform. But what is 'stage prescence' exactly? Is it the same thing for every singer? Or does it vary depending on the singer's personality?

Stage Presence: the ability to command the attention of an audience by the impressiveness of manner or appearance.

Stage Presence refers to the certain charisma and charm that a performer possesses that draws in an audience and commands their full attention. We can say that this can be partly dependant on the musical style in how it can be delivered though. There are in fact many different ways stage prescence can be projected by you as a performer and the trick is finding out or discovering what works for you.

Let's take some examples from popular Singers in various genres of music. Let these artistes provoke your imagination and inspire you;

Sam Cooke - *was an accomplished Gospel singer turned Pop/Soul artiste and he could stand flat-footed on stage using just his expressive singing and gestures as he held the microphone. He projected supreme confidence in his expression of the songs, his lips pouting and eyes flashing charmingly and intensely. He portrayed sheer confidence in his expression and his gestures and the audience loved him for it. Women and girls screamed and fainted in the Churches as his Gospel group, the Soul Stirrers performed*

Little Richard - *Flashed his fierce smile with eyes open wide as he pumped the keys of that piano. He astonished and excited his audiences with his larger than life personality and outrageous stage antics. A great innovator and he influenced so many great artistes, as he still does today. He made the best Rock n' Roll records. The architect of Rock n Roll!*

Elvis Presley - *Bumped and swivelled his hips on stage on The Ed Sullivan show in the fifties when you just couldn't do that, creating great controversy. He moved like no-one else just by feeling the music and Rock n' Roll went global! Elvis looked dangerous on stage and was a white man singing black music. Audiences didn't know what he was going to do next and his dynamic stage prescence shot him to international stardom.*

James Brown - *They called him Mister Dynamite. The Godfather of Soul, James Brown could sing with such raw energy and expression shouting 'Please, please please!' into the mic as he dropped to his knees with great theatrics . He could really dance! He would shuffle and glide across the stage like nobody before him. He introduced the funk with hypnotic grooves and syncopated vocals.*

Otis Redding - *Otis was a raw power-house of Soul. His vocal dynamics ranged from soft and husky to raucous and powerful. He stomped and dominated with towering prescence on the stage and his warm and* passionate delivery always brought the best out of his band and his audience.

Janis Joplin - *In the sixties, Janis was one of the first to make it acceptable for a woman to truly express herself in a raw and exposed way on-stage. Her expressive voice ranged from beautiful to banshee-like as she cryed, shrieked and screamed her way through her performances like a woman possessed to reveal her very soul.*

Robert Plant - *Standing statuesque, mic in hand, leaning back in rock posture, as his body contorted gracefully to the funk-rock guitar-heavy rhythms of Led Zeppelin. With his soaring, distinctive, dynamic vocals. Robert Plant projected a well defined image for seventies rock that has been much imitated over decades.*

Paul Rodgers - *One of the first to use a mic stand as an effective onstage prop. Throwing the mic stand high into the air and catching it at Hammermith Apollo Theatre. Impressive throw and catch. I tried it myself a few times successfully but stopped for a while after I nearly decapitated a trumpet player and hit the bass player in his forehead with the microphone.*

Morrissey - *Lamenting sorrowful and poetic lyrics whilst wearing flowers protruding from his hind-quarters. Absolute genius!*

Freddie Mercury - *Masterfully strided across the stage, using exaggerated and graceful theatrics. He endearingly referred to his audience as 'my beauties' and taunted the audience with magnificent and skillful call and response singing. He is still revered as the ultimate frontman.*

Michael Jackson - *Perfected dynamic dance moves and onstage choreographed dancing which set a new era in music video history and gave us the now iconic 'moonwalk.' The King of Pop was always dedicated to absolute perfection in his singing, music and his performance.*

Madonna - *An icon and a role model for women, Madonna, seduced her audiences spectacularly and helped re-define sexual freedom and* *taboo's with her showmanship and talent to re-invent herself theatrically onstage.*

Prince - *Prince cultivated magnificent presence onstage using both mysterious yet seductively magnetic and dynamic expressions. He also acted as a fantastic mime onstage, a master musician, exaggerating his movements. He didn't have to say barely a word as his terrific dance moves and dynamic music thrilled his audience, yet his vocals were also distinctive and dynamic.*

Alanis Morrisette - *When Alanis appeared on the music scene she sang deeply expressive and authentically raw and uninhibited songs in a way that many could identify with. Onstage in her body she expressed herself with the same intense, wild and free abandon as she ran across the stage, her body translating the feverish writhing intensity of the music.*

Jessie J - *Jessie is an artiste who expresses herself with fierce abandon and much freedom in her singing, dancing and stage performance. She is fearless in making every mannar of facial expression and extreme animated movements in her dynamic performances.*

Things you can do

1. Realise that it's not all about you anymore - It's all really about your audience.

2. Be well rehearsed. This shows an audience you're really serious and about your craft and professional.

3. Give the people what they want, musically. Also give them really quality entertainment.

4. Jump out of your comfort zone. Try new things to keep it your singing performance fresh and exciting.

5. Channel your fierce inner confidence. During your performance, be a leader. When the host is determined and confident, everyone follows suit. So be the pied piper musician and encourage your audience to follow you.

Ways to develop Stage Presence

1) Make sure you 'love' the songs you're singing! If not, you can come across as fake. In-authentic. An audience wants to believe that you have your heart in the songs you're singing. Express that to them. Just as we said earlier with interpretation of a cover song. Understand your lyric, feel it and express it.

2) Smile! At least occasionally. Even the most moody rock bands flash a smile occasionally. Let the audience know you're happy to be there and you're happy that they're there too. A smile on-stage looks amazing every time so don't hold back. You don't have to smile constantly like a deranged person but then again acting a little crazy or being crazy can have a great stage presence. Hats off to Ozzy Osbourne and all who follow his lead.

3) Move! Standing on the spot for the whole gig is a little boring and makes an audience feel like they could have stayed home with their feet up listening to a CD instead. Movement onstage is the main thing that sets live music apart from recorded music. HOW you move is up to you to decide and take guide from the music. In my first guitar band we started rooted to the floor but soon began to take notice what other bands were doing. Guitar players can swing your guitars as you rock out in unison. You can even choreograph simple movements with the guitars to great effect. Steal some moves if you like. When I eventually focused on being a frontman I even learned some of James Brown's moves (to the best of my ability) and later learned some Northern Soul dance moves that helped changed the dynamics of the performance and it became even more fun.

4) Talk to the audience - Create rapport with your audience. You might have to figure out how to do that in your own style. Express your personality and any background about the music or your passion for a song, or if you wrote it, express the idea behind it... when you wrote it, where you wrote it and why. Sometimes talking about everyday things can warm up an audience but don't talk for too long because they're really there for the music. You don't have to tell jokes and not everyone has the same sense of humour. One thing you do have in common is

the music and hopefully that why they're still there so enthuse them about the origin of the music when you talk to them. Make them feel involved with you and your music and thank them for being there. You see, it's all about the audience.

If you're still stuck for inspiration on how to develop more stage prescence, then watch what other performers you admire are doing. Can you include some of that same magic in your own performance? Or maybe you prefer to simply loosen up your own unique, un-immitatible personality. Set yourself free with the music and ... do it, *your* way!

Chapter Eight

Style Techniques

In this chapter we're going to cover stylistic techniques which can translate across many genres of music. Each of these is fundamental for contemporary singers in many styles. They add a technical polish and more expression to your singing and enable you to improvise more, bringing more flexibility to your singing and more stylistic effects in your performance.

The Note-bend - The note-bend is the most basic element of stylistic vocal phrasing. This is stepping up from one note to another and back down to the original note.

Try singing a note, starting on say, an F and bending the note up to G (a whole tone) and back down to F . (So you sing F-G-F)

This should sound like a short stutter of the tone up to G and back and you need to 'step it' rather than slurring the note up and back. Once you feel you've mastered this try it faster and with other notes going up in range.

This note-bend also works in the other direction so try singing down a tone and back as well. So in effect you're now singing G-F-G, for example. Again, the 'step-down' to the F here is a quick flick, change of pitch and you return immediately to the orginal pitch (G). Once you have mastered this quick stepping between pitches, practice speeding up the note-bend on higher pitches.

Trill - A trill is made up of three notes sung together quickly as one complete phrase. Trills are very common and they add a really professional and expressive style to the end of a phrase. There are Trill-downs and upward Trills.

Trill-down - Sing these notes together as a triplet. A-G-F. As before, be sure to 'step' the notes and not slur them so that the delineation between the notes is precise and not sloppy.

Once you have successfully sung this a few times, work at speeding it up without slurring the notes. Keep 'stepping it' but sing as one phrase, smoothly as possible. Next sing the trill-down three times in a row as a loop. Repeat this, gradually moving up to higher pitches.

Listen to songs which use 'Trill-down' at the end of each line. A great example of this is Otis Redding's 'Sittin' on the Dock of the Bay.' Notice how he uses the trill-down, singing three notes together quickly in succession on 'bay' and 'a-way.'

Upward Trill - Sing these notes together as a triplet. F-G-A. As before, be sure to 'step' the notes and not slur them so that the delineation between the notes is precise and not sloppy.

It can be a bit trickier singing an upward trills compared with a Trill-down but if you practice it repetitively you will master it with smoothly delineation the same as with a Trill-down.

Trills are used in Blues, Soul and R&B extensively although you'll find them used to great effect in most Rock and Pop music also.

Crying on Pitch

Crying on pitch is effective and emotive. When an actor is reflecting sadness in their voice, talking in a sorrowful or emotive way, this is the same effect except we translate this to singing. A crying or whining quality is a physical change of the larynx, a tilt of the thyroid cartilage which shortens the vocal folds, giving you more flexibility to hit higher notes more easily. It also sounds great and is used in all styles of music. variation of the tonal quality can be achieved with higher or lower larynx height to brighten or darken your tone into a sob. Refer back to our Body section on Voice qualities to experiment and practice using this technique and have fun with it.

Disconnect to Falsetto

You may hear this used as a stylistic effect more commonly in Country and Folk singing yet it can be heard in many styles as well as Pop and Soul. It can sound a bit like a yodel but also in a ballad it can be really effective and sound amazing.

It's the effect that can be heard when a singer sings a phrase in their chest or mix register and then disconnects from that full tone (during the phrase) into a light, breathy, sometimes high pitched falsetto quality.

This is a really excellent dynamic technique because it quickly shifts your voice quality into a more subtle tone and when done well it sounds beautiful to the listener.

To practice this disconnect technique, experiment with changing your tone between a full bodied chest tone and a breathy falsetto tone within the same phrase. You might want to find examples of songs or singers who do this to refine this as a skill. It's a vocal cords switch from thick cords to thin, where your folds are vibrating on just the edges to create the breathy disconnected tone where we hear more of the airflow than

181

the tone itself. So for example the ratio of 'airflow to tone' might be something like 80:20. 80% air and 20% tone quality.

Experiment

I encourage you to try to experiment with a range of stylistic techniques. There are many and naturally some of them are more commonly used in specific styles but don't let the idea of these various session styles of music limit you. Take some risks stylistically and you can paint your music on a much broader canvas. Simply use stylistic effects that you enjoy and that add interesting dynamics to your singing.

We are each usually drawn to our personal favourite styles of music yet variety and diversity is what makes the world go around. Trying a vocal style of music that you don't usually sing can be very rewarding because you learn something new each time and you pull another style into your repertoire that you can draw upon and sometimes integrate into your personal style for surprisingly creative and exciting results.

So if you're a Rock singer, try Reggae and if you do Screamo, mix it up with some Jazz and enjoy your Reggae/Rock and Screamo/Jazz fusion.

Chapter Nine

Effortless Mastery

There is a level of mastery that many singers or artistes work to achieve where they can perform in a way that appears effortless. Some have called this being 'in the flow.' Being in the flow refers to the ability to maintain a balance of relaxation and focus in your performance.

This 'in the flow' is a certain state that a performer can access which is a point of awareness that sits between 'the relaxation zone' and 'pure intention of focus' and enables a performer to achieve their best performances. This will be especially useful to you if you tend to over-think your performance and therefore struggle with relaxing and expressing yourself.

To enable you to achieve this ideal state you need to:

1) Practice and exercise your voice fully to the point that your singing becomes second nature and you don't need to think about it...You become instinctive.

2) Let go into your *creative impulse* when you're performing. Sing from a flexible and malleable place of creation and expression.

3) Access the meditative state of Alpha where muscle relaxation is combined with a light mindfulness so you are completely 'in the zone' with the music. See the earlier chapter on meditation.

When you're in this state, the practice you have already done has built the co-ordination into your muscle memory. Getting out of your mind and Letting go to the music opens up your flexibility and freedom to respond to the music and create freely in the moment.

Accessing the meditative alpha state where you are relaxed yet focused enables your singing to have a precise yet effortless flow where your muscles respond with ease and freedom to the demands of the music.

The purpose of this is to get 'out of your mind' and into 'the space' or 'the zone.' This idea is the basis of Kenny Werner's excellent book Effortless Mastery.

Sometimes when you care 'too much' about singing well it can lead to sabotage through an urge to perform well. It can help you greatly to form a habit of being completely in the present moment with the music so that you can feel that 'connection' to the music... a connection to everything that many musicians call 'the space' or 'the zone.' It's also sometimes known as the 'Soul' space where the best performances come from because many recognise it as being a deep spiritual connection. It's a place where powerful performances come from.

Thinking 'too much' about your singing is a form of sabotage because too many thoughts from the conscious mind have an analytical agenda which ultimately holds you back from being free with your singing.

So, the goal of effortless mastery is to firstly practice well mindfully and consciously but when you are confident enough with the piece of music you need to GET OUT of your mind and into 'the space.'

This 'space' or 'zone' has no restrictive agenda. It is purely emotive and expressive and allows a real sense of 'flow' into a performance.

A large part of accessing this state is in developing your deep breathing which enables you to relax your body. Practicing the exercises on Meditation given earlier in this book will help to achieve this. Also, you can find many good examples on the internet. Let's break this down as a technique:

1) Practice well, so you have anchored the song into your muscle memory.

2) Next LET GO of your thoughts and breath deeply into the creative space.

3) Access the meditative state where you feel connected with only the music...

This is the relaxed, yet focused place we call 'in the zone.'

The Complete Vocalist Process

So, Finally let's combine Mind, Body and Soul as a three step process that you can integrate into your singing, songs and your entire performance. You can seize more control over your mindset, your voice and express yourself much more authentically using this process. Simply absorbing the knowledge, ideas and techniques in this book will inspire and enrich you although it's through practicing this as a process and applying it to your singing that you'll reap the full rewards which will show up as focus, ability and passion in your performance.

At the beginning of this book I referred to Mind, Body & Soul as the three point system. These three elements when combined inspire great vocal performances. Making a practice of using this process and including techniques in this book to prepare for rehearsals, sessions and gigs will integrate all three naturally into your performance. Be curious, be creative, adventurous and enjoy this freedom to express yourself to make the very best of your singing.

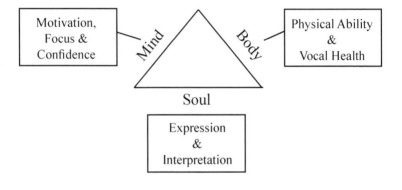

Step One - Mindset

Close your eyes: Visualise and repeat the number 3, three times.

This is level 3 for physical relaxation, Deep, Slow Breathing. Relax different parts of your body, starting with your head and work your way down to your toes.

Visualise and repeat the Number 2, three times - Visualise a tranquil scene. Feel fully composed and relaxed of mind.

Visualise and repeat the Number 1, three times This is the basic plain level … Where you can program your subconscious mind.

Close your eyes and Project a movie screen in your mind - You will create three scenes:

1) Project an image on the screen. Visualise yourself, as you are today (with your excitement in what you're embarking upon with your own singing. With any fears you have of performing).

2) Move the movie scene to the left and change the colour of the frame to blue. Now visualise yourself working on your voice, working on songs, practicing, recording yourself.

3) Change the frame of the screen to white. Now visualise yourself performing to an audience. You are on a stage. See the positive reaction of the audience. You are enjoying the moment, leading the song. You are so immersed in the song, telling the story and the music itself. The song is the only thing that's truly important and the audience hang upon your every word… because your song, the song you are singing is also 'their song' and they feel it as you do as the words and notes leave your lips. They feel the vibration of the music and the power of the meaning in the words you're singing. Add any details that are important to you to complete the scene to your desire.

Anchor this Point of Reference (pinching three fingers together, access that feeling) and in doing so anchor in the confidence of knowing everything is happening perfectly as you intended it.

This psycho-motor rehearsal works like rocket fuel for confidence.

Step Two - Body

Here is an example of a great routine I can recommend. Use the exercises below in the order given as there is a progression that will enable a gradual and effective Vocal warm-up without adding any excess tension or strain. The main thing is that it's important to 'stay loose' so your body is not uptight or tense.

1) Let go of any undue tension by doing a gentle body warm-up with stretches and relax your neck and shoulders.

2) Take low, deep breaths to relax your body and gain composure.

3) Exercise Routine: Use the following to various scales: Five tone, Octaves, Circular scale (1.5 Octave), Major/Minor, Siren or another of your choice.

Lip Roll - Place your thumb and forefinger either side of your lips on each cheek where dimples sometimes form and lift the skin slightly. Pout your lips a little and make a spoken letter 'B' position with your lips. Take a low breath and as you exhale blow air through your lips. Notice how your lips vibrate loosely. Now make this same sound to the pitch of a scale or siren. The Circular scale we mentioned earlier is ideal for this. Underneath the 'Lip roll' focus on a dopey 'Uh' to keep your larynx relaxed and allow your cords to naturally make pitch.

Tone Builders (Mmm, Nng) - Say 'Mm' edgily as if enthusiastically responding to great smelling food. This is like a hum but just slightly edgier. Use this to scales or melodies. Also use 'Ng' as in the word 'sing' and keep this high tongue position as you sing scales or melodies.

Balance - (Gug, Gee, Goo) Say each of these or combination of all three with a well-articulated 'G.' Again use scales or melodies.

Mix (Nei) - Say the word 'Nei' or 'Nay-ee.' Add 'Crying'on pitch or a whiny quality and sing a circular scale or specific song melodies. Replace your song lyrics with 'Nei' to develop your mix.

Muh - Say the word 'Muh' or 'Mum.' Dig into the 'M' consonant for compression and stability. Sing this to an octave or circular scale or another scale of your choice. Then sing the same scale again with just the vowell, without the 'M' consonant. Finally sing it again sustaining just one note to a crescendo and control it to a decresendo.

Alternatively you can create or practice your own personal vocal warm-up and exercise routine that you use regularly and especially before a rehearsal or live performance. If you have a Voice coach, ask them to help you design a tailored routine or get some SLS training to facilitate an appropriate routine that caters for your own style. There will be some exercises that are more effective for some singers than others and it depends upon the singer's own requirement, tend-to's and whatever is the goal of their specific vocal style but make sure it's a progressive warm-up or exercise routine that warms your voice gently before your muscles and cords are warm enough to sing 'wide open.'

Step Three - Soul

Close your eyes and listen to the music. Pay close attention to how it makes you feel. What feelings does it conjure up? Longing, sadness, pain, happiness, bliss, hope? Stay with the feelings as the music washes over you. When a feeling becomes very intense pinch your three fingers together to anchor this as a point of reference.

Walking through this process of listening to the music and anchoring in these feelings will enable you more direct communication of expression and will deepen your relationship with the song and the music. In a sense you become one with the song and develop a meaningful relationship with it. Allowing yourself to feel these deep feelings will enable you to anchor them in and re-visit them each time you perform the song. This works in the same way as a 'method actor' plays a particular part by 'living' through the thoughts and feelings of a character. You are absorbing the heartfelt meaning of the music and interpreting it with your own voice. This may sound trite to some but without this deep expression a song is just words and music. It has no soul.

If you're singing your own song that you've written that has special meaning for you and particularly if the feelings were raw and authentic then expressing these emotions will be easier because you have a direct reference to the meaning behind the song. You have experienced it first hand and lived it!! So, you cannot fail to express it. Tell the story from your point of view as though you're telling someone for the first time.

Keep singing and have great adventures.